ORIGAMI
FOR BEGINNERS

Vicente Palacios

DOVER PUBLICATIONS, INC.
Mineola, New York

Bibliographical Note

This Dover edition, first published in 1999, includes all diagrams and an English translation of all instructions published in *Papiroflexia fácil* by Editorial Miguel A. Salvatella, Barcelona, Spain, in 1995. Omitted from the Dover edition are the original Publisher's Note, an essay on the history of origami, and a list of origami associations. The author's Introduction has been shortened. Figures that appeared in color in the original edition have been reproduced here in black and white. This Dover edition is published by special arrangement with Editorial Miguel A. Salvatella S. A.

Library of Congress Cataloging-in-Publication Data

Palacios, Vicente.
     Origami for beginners / Vicente Palacios.
          p.   cm.
     Abridged translation of: Papiroflexia facil.
     ISBN 0-486-40284-3 (pbk.)
     1. Origami.   I. Title.
TT870.P28   1999
736'.982—dc21   98-42549
                                                                          CIP

Manufactured in the United States of America
Dover Publications, Inc., 31 East 2nd Street, Mineola, N.Y. 11501

CONTENTS

Introduction	4	Pinwheel	36
Symbols	6	Checked Box 5	38
Cap	7	Triangular Box with Cover	39
Inclined Pyramid	8	Checked Box 6	40
Cube 1	9	Box-Table	41
Cube 2	10	Tall Box with Cover	42
Cube 3	11	Basket	44
Triangular Box	12	Rotated Box 1	46
Cap with Visor	13	Five-Pointed Star	48
Cube 4	14	Eight-Pointed Star 2	50
Airplane	15	Star with Wings	51
Vase	16	Rotor	52
Four-Pointed Star	17	Modular Wheel	53
Checked Box 1	18	Easter Dish	54
Checked Box 2	19	The Little Bird	55
Checked Box 3	20	Display Case	56
Imprisoned Cube 1	21	Eight-Sided Box	58
Imprisoned Cube 2	22	Six-Sided Box with Cover	60
Imprisoned Cube 3	23	Ten-Sided Box	62
Checked Box 4	24	Whistle That Whistles	63
Eight-Pointed Star 1	25	Cinderella's Shoe	64
Little-Birds Cube	26	Gyroscope 1	66
Squares within Octagon	27	Gyroscope 2	68
Little Mama Bird	28	Multicolor Star	70
Stool	29	Rotated Box 2 and Three Variants	71
Five-Sided Coaster 1	30	Double Measure	74
Eight-Segment Rosette	31	Three-Dimensional Star	76
Rotated Coaster	32	Vampire Bat	77
Six-Sided Coaster	33	Flowerpot	80
Centerpiece Holder	34		

ORIGAMI

Origami is the creation of figures with a recognizable meaning, by means of the geometric folding of a sheet of paper, which preferably is square.

This art developed in the East from the idea of "creation from nothing." With minimal resources, accessible to everyone, one tries to create the most beautiful, or well realized, or ambitious figures, by means of some folds always or almost always "fixed." Folding techniques are continually advancing.

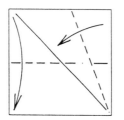

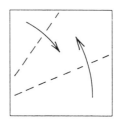

In fixed folding, an edge or corner of the paper is brought to another edge or corner, or to a line that passes through the paper's center.

Arbitrary folding is random in terms of where the fold is placed.

Fixed folding is genuine folding. Arbitrary folding is accepted as a rare recourse; abuse of arbitrary folding would detract interest, in principle, from a figure, and it would be very difficult to make it the same way again without taking measurements, or memorizing the process of folding it.

Of course, it is possible to fold a lion's head and not the complete lion from a paper, or to form the body later and join the two figures to form the complete animal. In such a case, the final figure would be a composite of two simple creations. In the same way, one can fold some geometric elements, the same or different in form, so that, put together, they form an ensemble or a modular figure.

What significance has a module? In itself, it may or may not represent something, but the final composition, though it may be a purely geometric figure, reveals the significance of its distinct elements. They are parts of a whole.

Is it preferable to make a figure with a single paper, or with several papers? It is impossible to say! They are two different things. If the final result has the same form and complexity, clearly it would be preferable to make the figure with a single paper.

What type of paper should you use? Not only the type of paper, but also the size of that paper, depends on the specific case. Some figures will turn out well in one size and badly in another. Each paperfolder, in accordance with personal judgment and taste, should employ the paper that seems likely to provide the best results. Some figures require a fine paper, while others demand a thick paper. If you don't have a clear idea of what type or size of paper will be most suitable for folding a figure, the best thing to do is experiment, observe, compare.

When folding a figure for the first time, it is necessary to be very attentive to all the instructions. If one is overlooked, probably the figure will not be folded well. It is very important to know the meanings of the symbols or signs. On page 6 are listed all of them that commonly are used internationally. You always must fold with care and precision, because otherwise the final result may be disastrous.

The folding of a figure always is an exercise: sometimes of attentiveness, other times of observation, or of ingenuity to perform a step in the best way possible. Such exercises create habits, and thus some steps that in the beginning seem complicated later become easy to do. They enable you then to venture other, more difficult folds.

Later, setting out to create your own figures provides great satisfaction, and much more so if you obtain very good results. All kinds of methods are valid for creating a new figure. Sometimes, after repeatedly folding a figure, you will take a different path, in search of one that may be better. At other times you may start folding at random. You may also start by drawing the figure you are setting out to invent, and mentally diagramming each step in its creation. If at some point you don't know how to continue, it's all right to leave it for another time, or try by other means. Great successes rarely are achieved without considerable effort.

In the creation of a figure, it is very important that the final result be compact. It detracts a great deal if the figure is loose, or spreads out or unfolds by itself. If the figure is flat, it is important to take care that its back side is at least presentable. If the figure looks equally beautiful from either side, so much the better.

There are some figures—most of them simple—that have been repeated many times in the same way, or with minimal variations, and that are in common use, as the most traditional figures. The number of different figures that can be created is "mathematically infinite."

Origami leads people to communicate with other paperfolders, even in distant countries. Thus, it becomes a stimulus to learn other languages and to learn to draw better, given that drawing is the best way to transmit the process of folding a figure, and, of course, is an international "language." International origami conventions are organized in many countries. At the conventions, new figures are demonstrated in classes and in exhibitions. By attending, you can meet other origami enthusiasts, including some who are internationally renowned.

Many now-famous origami enthusiasts got their start in paperfolding after seeing, in childhood, an impressive figure folded from paper. That early glimpse of origami was enough to motivate them to begin and persevere in an art that they considered to be just right for them. I hope that many readers will see in this book much more than simple folded figures, and that it helps and inspires those already involved in origami to persevere, maintaining and promoting the "sacred fire" of this hobby.

Vicente Palacios

SYMBOLS

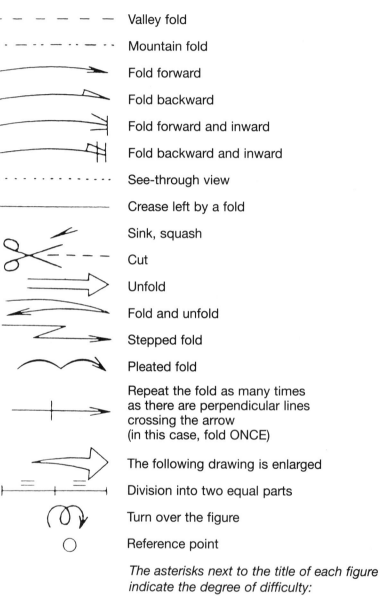

Valley fold

Mountain fold

Fold forward

Fold backward

Fold forward and inward

Fold backward and inward

See-through view

Crease left by a fold

Sink, squash

Cut

Unfold

Fold and unfold

Stepped fold

Pleated fold

Repeat the fold as many times
as there are perpendicular lines
crossing the arrow
(in this case, fold ONCE)

The following drawing is enlarged

Division into two equal parts

Turn over the figure

Reference point

*The asterisks next to the title of each figure
indicate the degree of difficulty:*

* = very easy

* * = easy

* * * = somewhat difficult

* * * * = more difficult

CAP
by Vicente Palacios

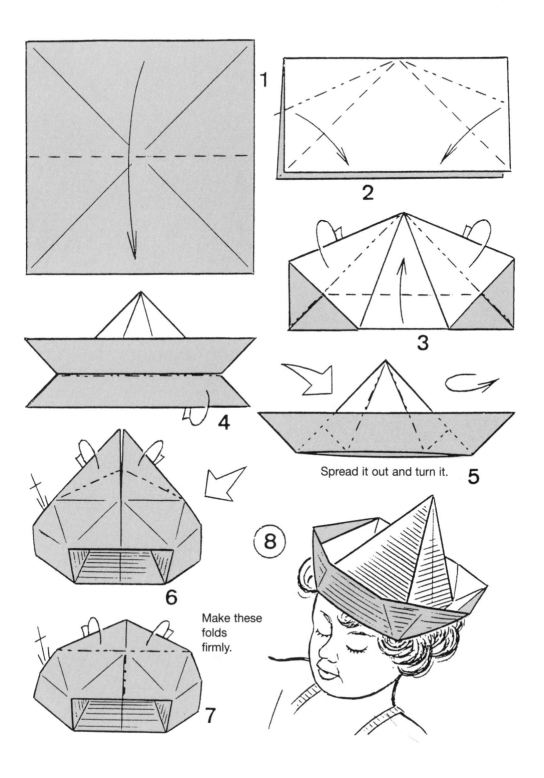

1

2

3

4

5

Spread it out and turn it.

6

Make these
folds
firmly.

7

8

INCLINED PYRAMID
by Francisco J. Caboblanco

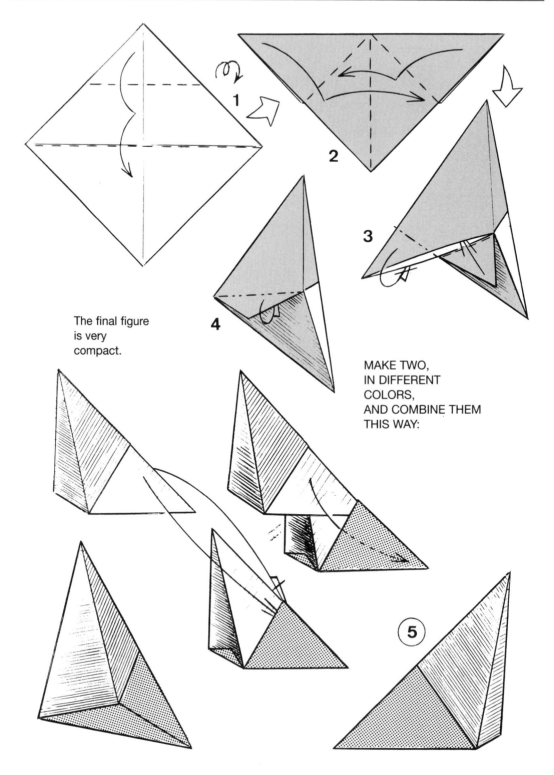

The final figure
is very
compact.

MAKE TWO,
IN DIFFERENT
COLORS,
AND COMBINE THEM
THIS WAY:

CUBE 1
by Miguel Ángel Palacios

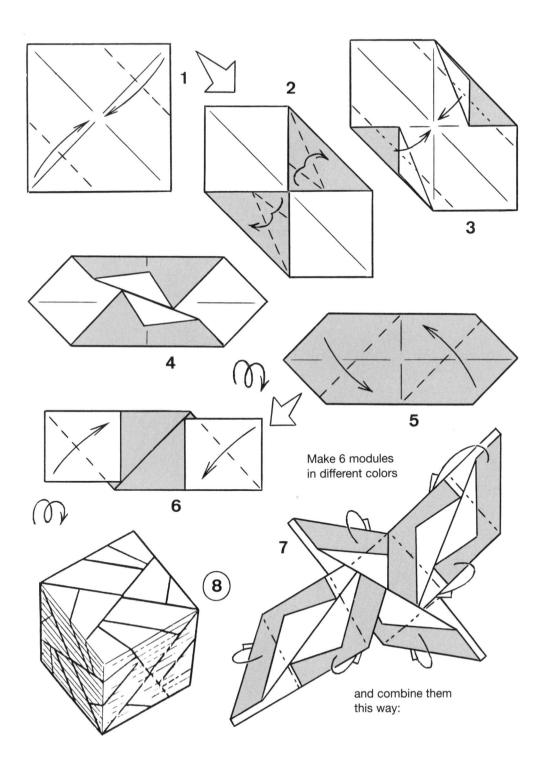

Make 6 modules
in different colors

and combine them
this way:

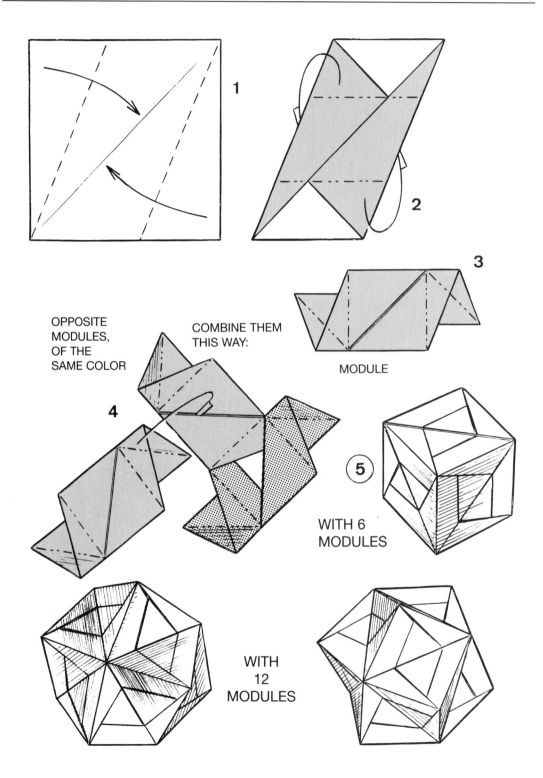

1

2

3

OPPOSITE
MODULES,
OF THE
SAME COLOR

COMBINE THEM
THIS WAY:

MODULE

4

(5)

WITH 6
MODULES

WITH
12
MODULES

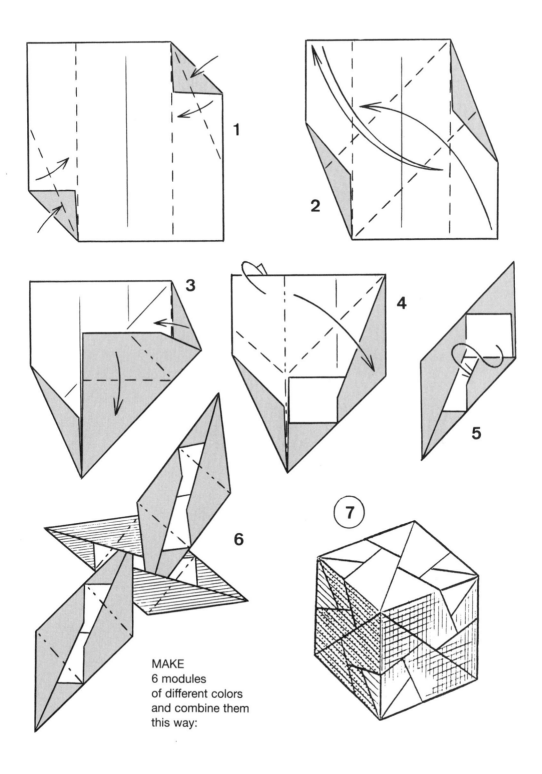

MAKE
6 modules
of different colors
and combine them
this way:

TRIANGULAR BOX
by Mirco Ulandi

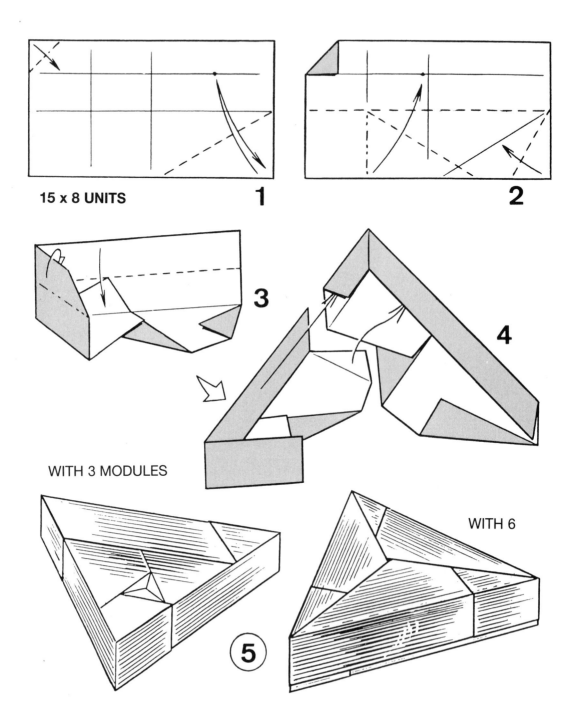

15 x 8 UNITS

1

2

3

4

WITH 3 MODULES

WITH 6

5

CAP WITH VISOR

This model is the result of successive improvements. One of them was published by Mrs. Kricskovics as the creation of Simon Jánosné Ovónö of Hungary.

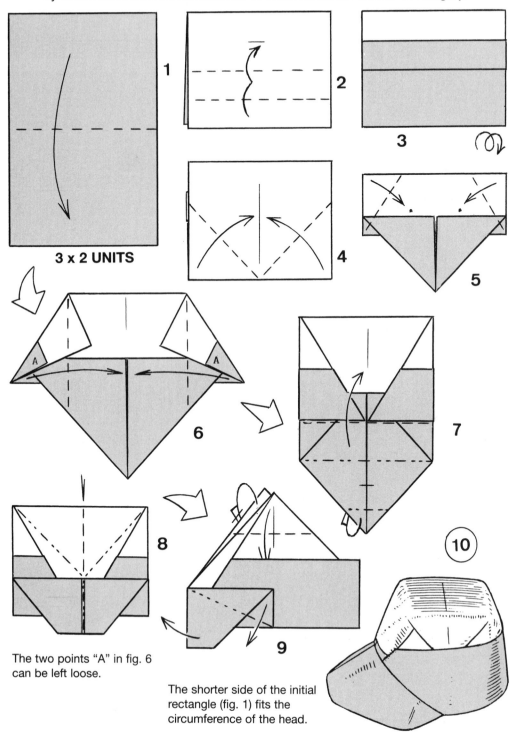

3 x 2 UNITS

The two points "A" in fig. 6 can be left loose.

The shorter side of the initial rectangle (fig. 1) fits the circumference of the head.

CUBE 4
by Francisco J. Caboblanco

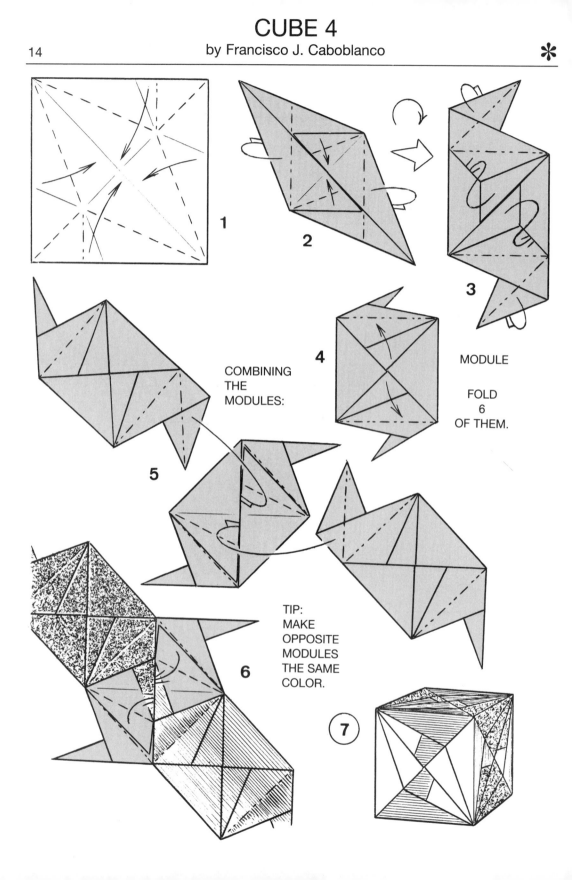

1

2

3

4

MODULE

FOLD
6
OF THEM.

COMBINING
THE
MODULES:

5

TIP:
MAKE
OPPOSITE
MODULES
THE SAME
COLOR.

6

7

AIRPLANE
by Yoshihide Momotani

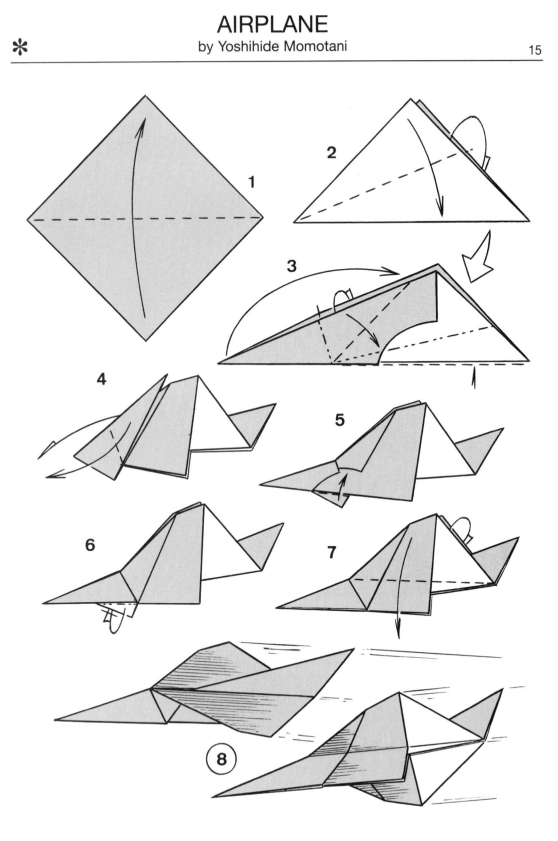

VASE

by Vicente Palacios (variant of those by Saburo Kase, T. Takahama, etc.) ✳

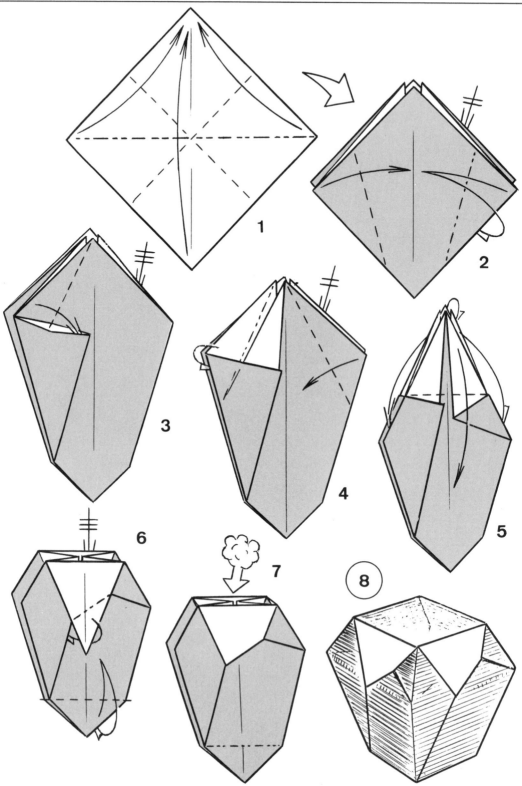

FOUR-POINTED STAR
by Vicente Palacios

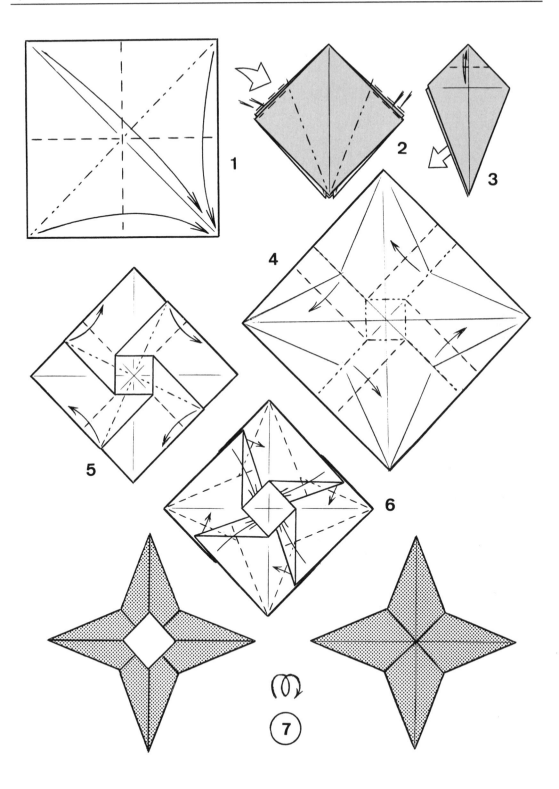

CHECKED BOX 1
by Francisco J. Caboblanco

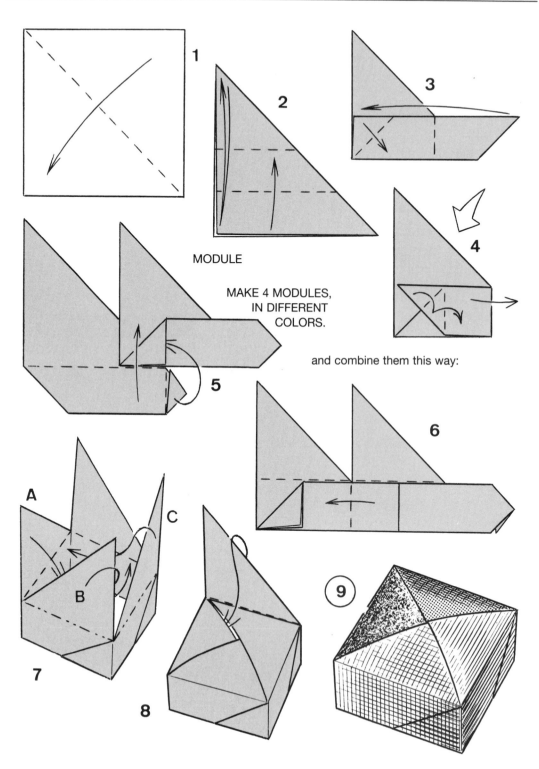

1

2

3

4

MODULE

MAKE 4 MODULES,
IN DIFFERENT
COLORS.

and combine them this way:

5

6

A

C

B

7

8

9

CHECKED BOX 2
by Francisco J. Caboblanco

＊＊

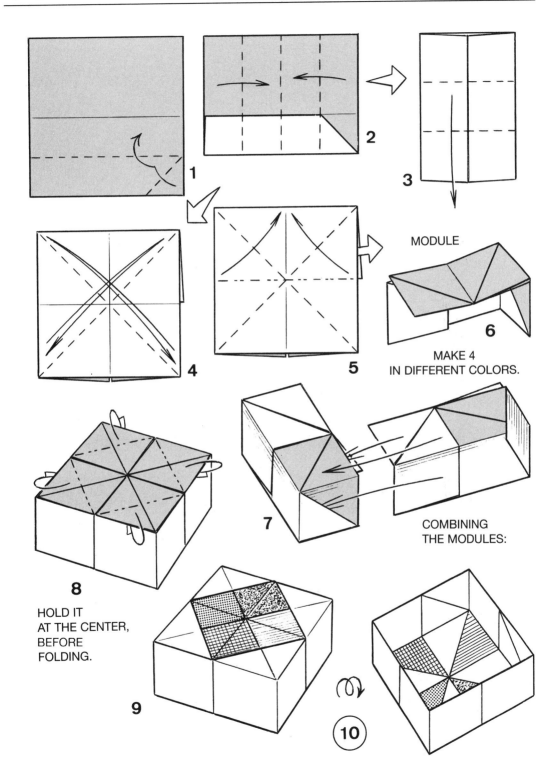

1

2

3

4

5

6

MODULE

MAKE 4
IN DIFFERENT COLORS.

7

**COMBINING
THE MODULES:**

8

HOLD IT
AT THE CENTER,
BEFORE
FOLDING.

9

10

CHECKED BOX 3
by Francisco J. Caboblanco

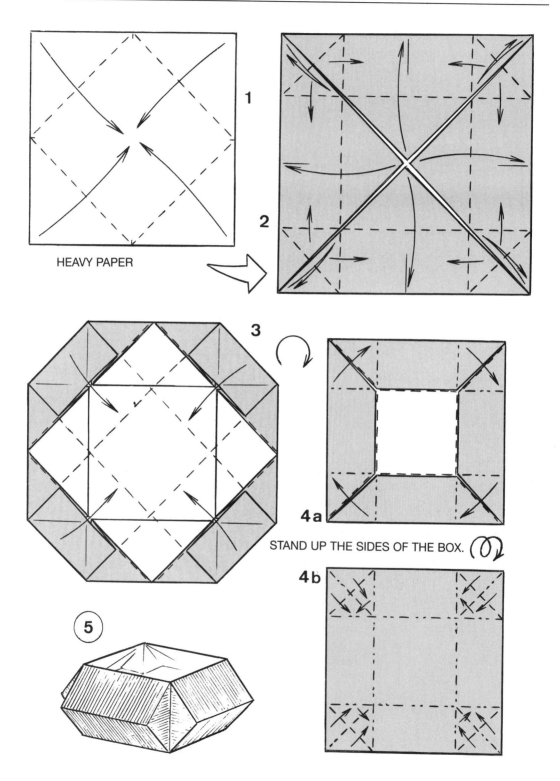

HEAVY PAPER

1

2

3

4a

STAND UP THE SIDES OF THE BOX.

4b

5

by Gabriel Pons

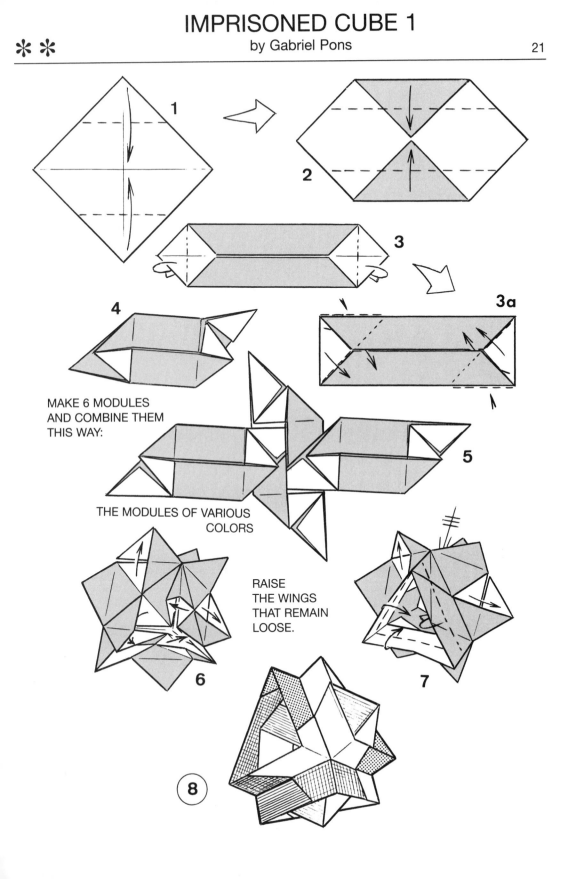

1

2

3

3a

4

MAKE 6 MODULES
AND COMBINE THEM
THIS WAY:

5

THE MODULES OF VARIOUS
COLORS

RAISE
THE WINGS
THAT REMAIN
LOOSE.

6

7

8

✳ ✳

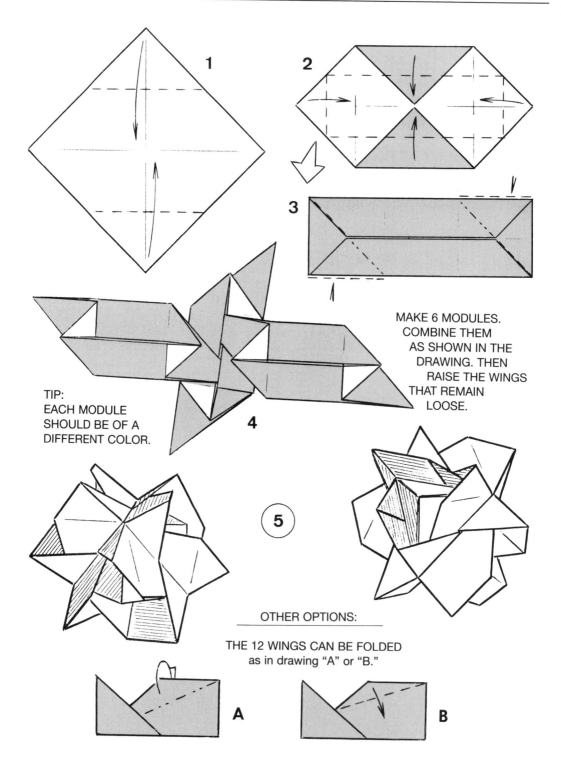

1

2

3

MAKE 6 MODULES.
COMBINE THEM
AS SHOWN IN THE
DRAWING. THEN
RAISE THE WINGS
THAT REMAIN
LOOSE.

TIP:
EACH MODULE
SHOULD BE OF A
DIFFERENT COLOR.

4

5

OTHER OPTIONS:

THE 12 WINGS CAN BE FOLDED
as in drawing "A" or "B."

A

B

IMPRISONED CUBE 3
by Miguel Ángel Palacios

✳ ✳

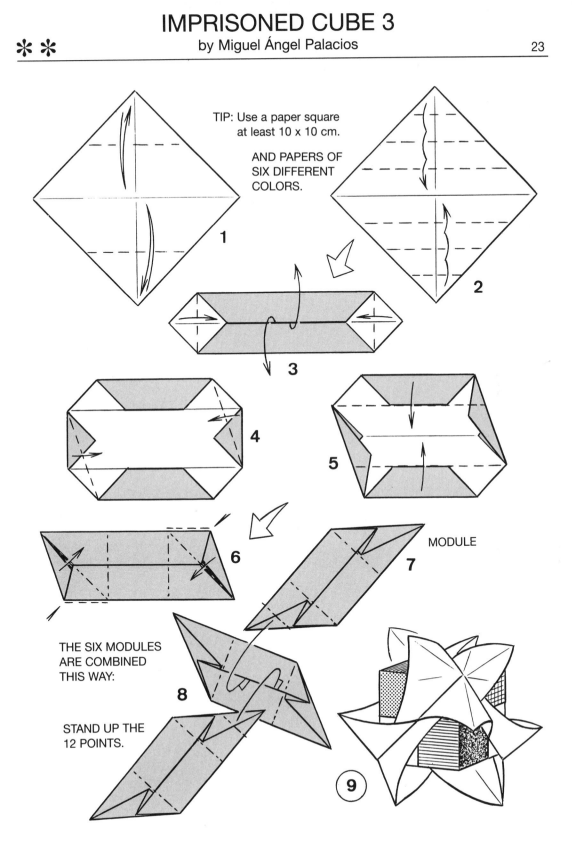

TIP: Use a paper square at least 10 x 10 cm.

AND PAPERS OF SIX DIFFERENT COLORS.

1

2

3

4

5

6

7

MODULE

THE SIX MODULES ARE COMBINED THIS WAY:

8

STAND UP THE 12 POINTS.

9

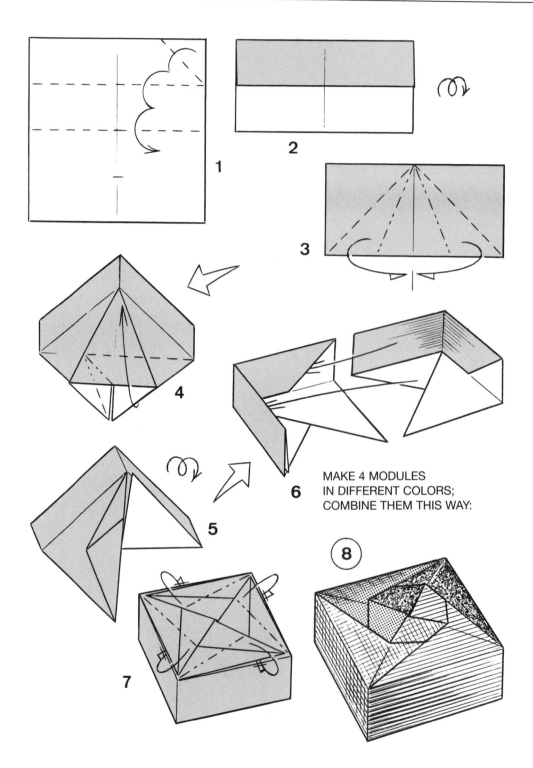

MAKE 4 MODULES
IN DIFFERENT COLORS;
COMBINE THEM THIS WAY:

✳ ✳

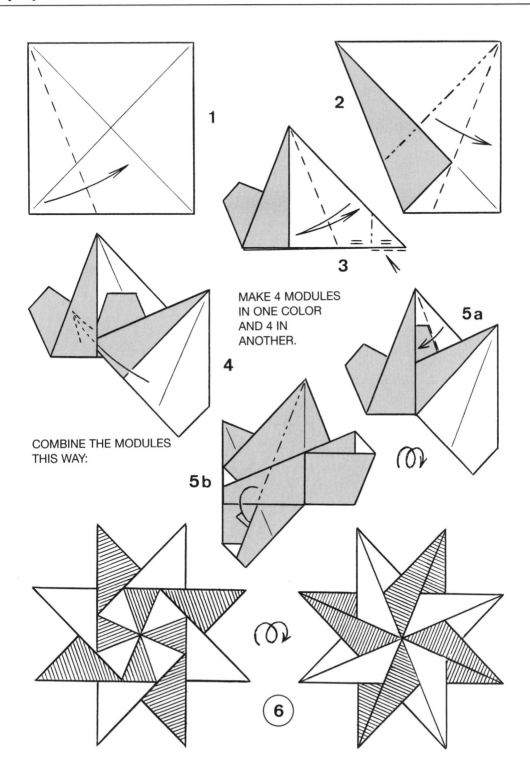

1

2

3

MAKE 4 MODULES
IN ONE COLOR
AND 4 IN
ANOTHER.

4

5a

COMBINE THE MODULES
THIS WAY:

5b

6

LITTLE-BIRDS CUBE
by Vicente Palacios

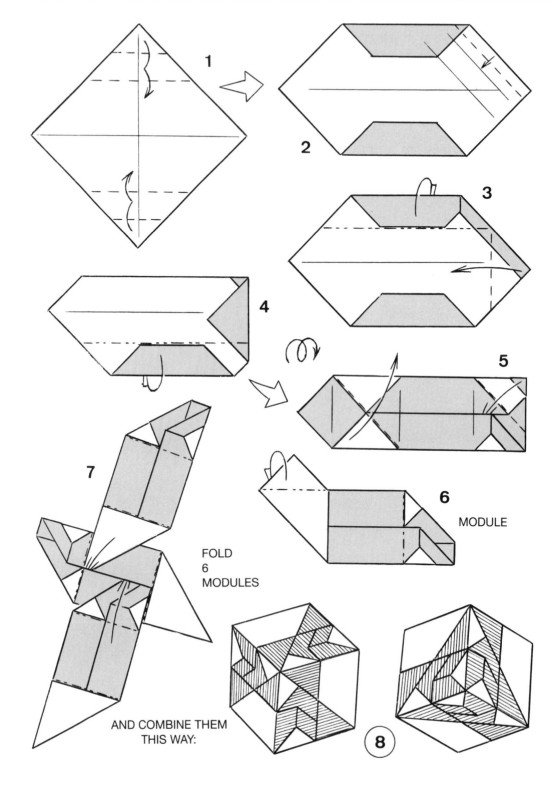

MODULE

FOLD
6
MODULES

AND COMBINE THEM
THIS WAY:

SQUARES WITHIN OCTAGON
by Francisco J. Caboblanco

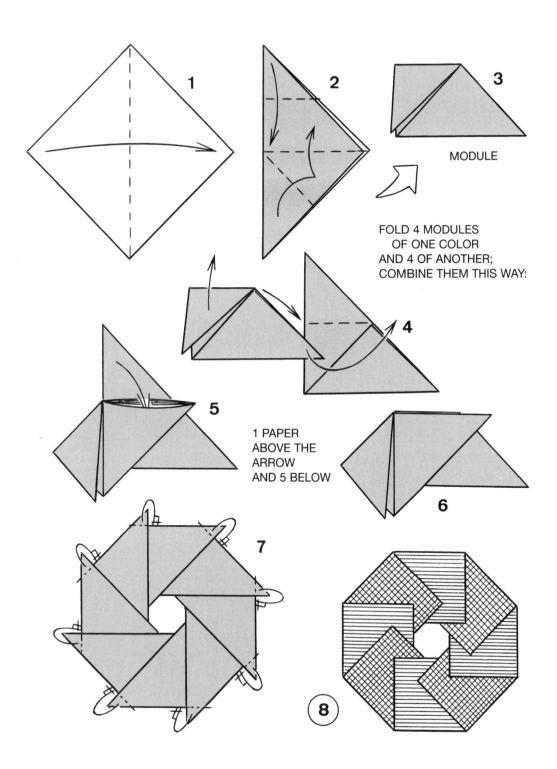

MODULE

FOLD 4 MODULES
OF ONE COLOR
AND 4 OF ANOTHER;
COMBINE THEM THIS WAY:

1 PAPER
ABOVE THE
ARROW
AND 5 BELOW

LITTLE MAMA BIRD
by Francis Ow

✳✳

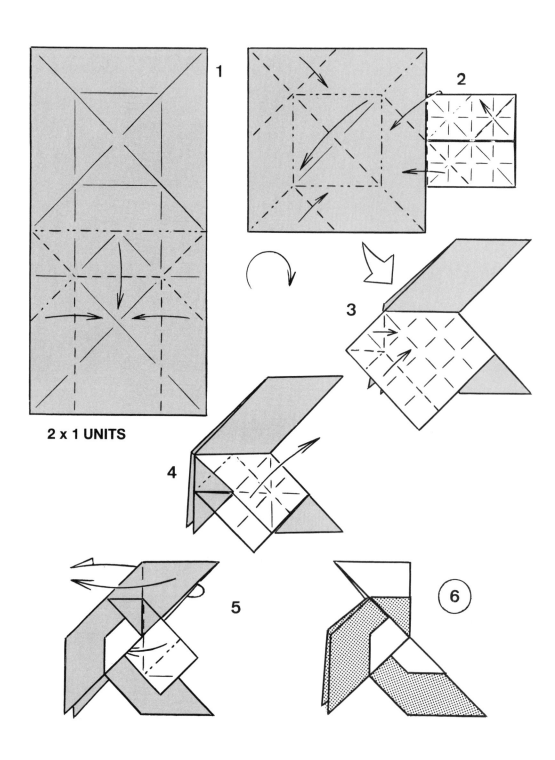

2 x 1 UNITS

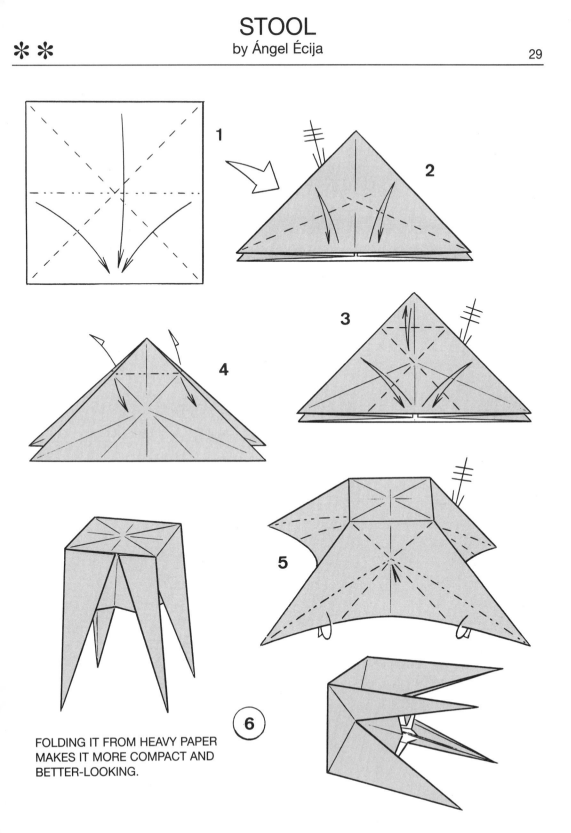

FOLDING IT FROM HEAVY PAPER
MAKES IT MORE COMPACT AND
BETTER-LOOKING.

FIVE-SIDED COASTER 1
by Francisco J. Caboblanco

** **

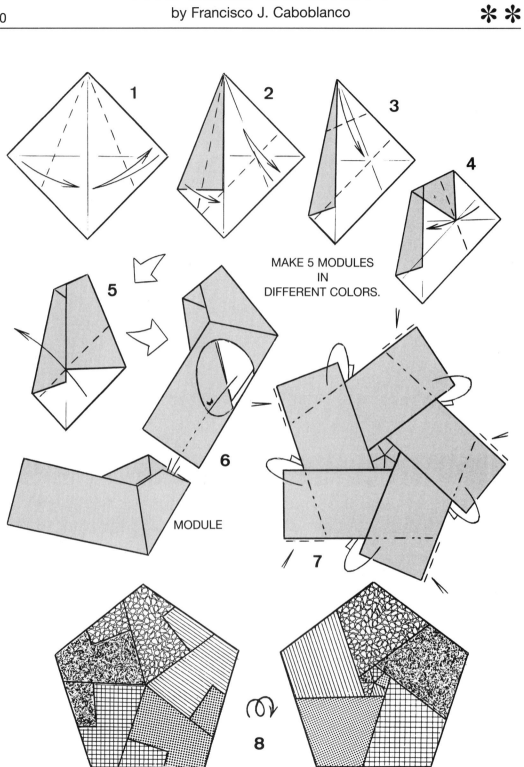

MAKE 5 MODULES
IN
DIFFERENT COLORS.

MODULE

EIGHT-SEGMENT ROSETTE
by Francisco J. Caboblanco

* *

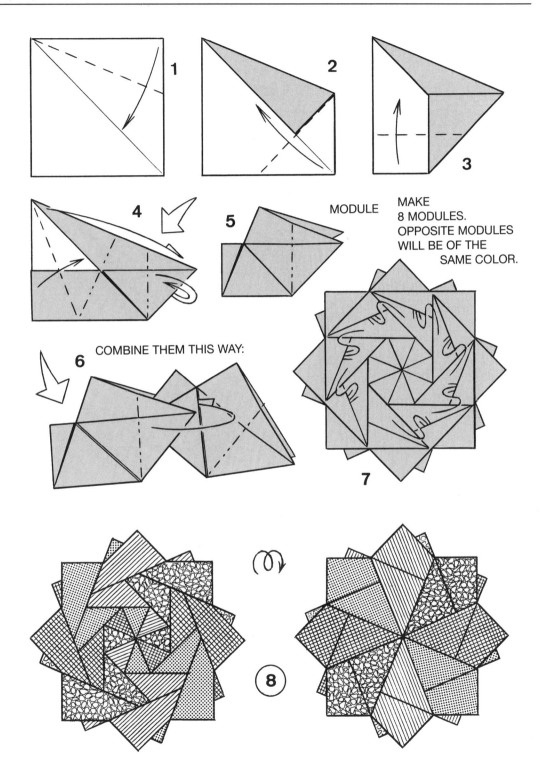

1

2

3

4

5

MODULE

MAKE 8 MODULES. OPPOSITE MODULES WILL BE OF THE SAME COLOR.

COMBINE THEM THIS WAY:

6

7

8

ROTATED COASTER
by Francisco J. Caboblanco

✳ ✳

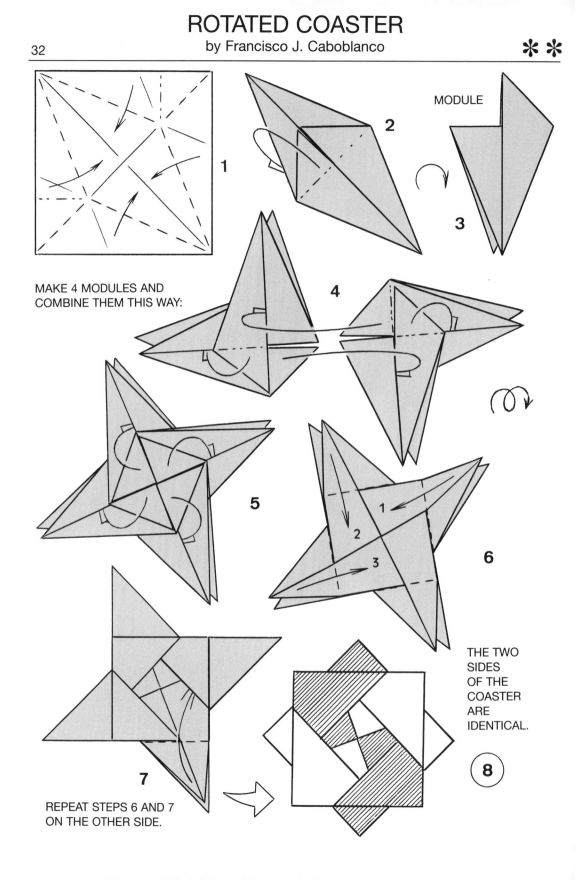

MODULE

MAKE 4 MODULES AND
COMBINE THEM THIS WAY:

THE TWO
SIDES
OF THE
COASTER
ARE
IDENTICAL.

REPEAT STEPS 6 AND 7
ON THE OTHER SIDE.

SIX-SIDED COASTER
by Francisco J. Caboblanco

✳ ✳ ✳

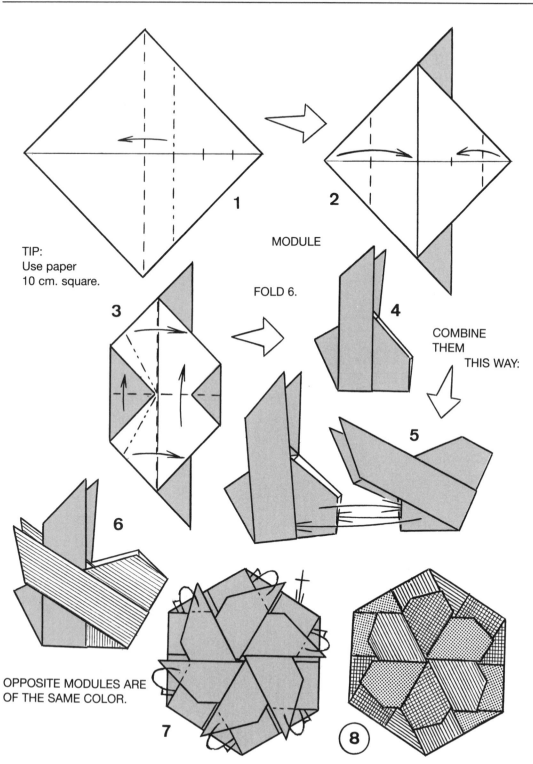

1

TIP:
Use paper
10 cm. square.

2

MODULE

FOLD 6.

3

4

COMBINE
THEM
THIS WAY:

5

6

OPPOSITE MODULES ARE
OF THE SAME COLOR.

7

8

CENTERPIECE HOLDER

by Miguel Ángel Palacios

✳ ✳ ✳

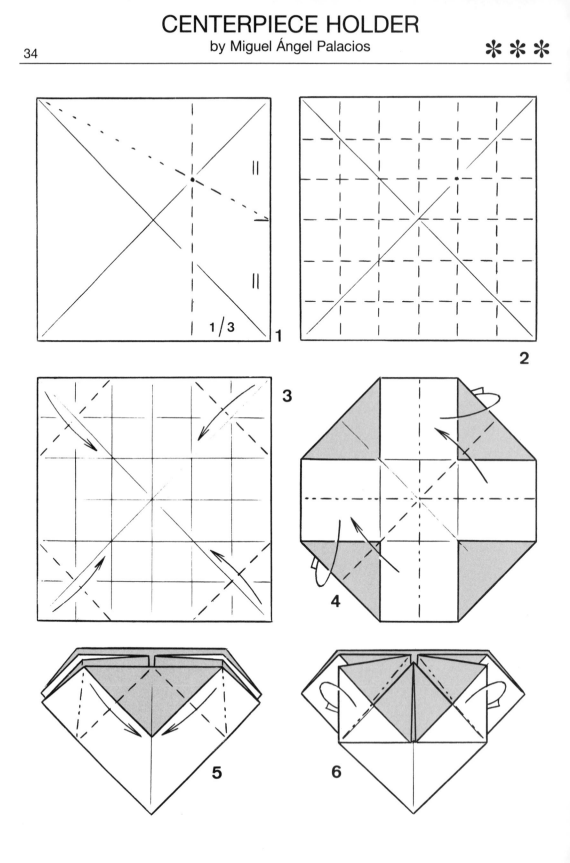

7

8

9

10

PINWHEEL
by Vicente Palacios

✳ ✳ ✳

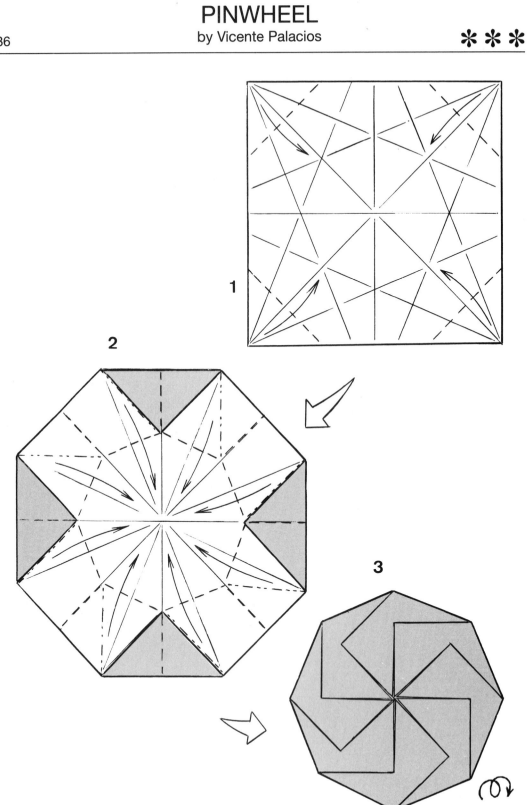

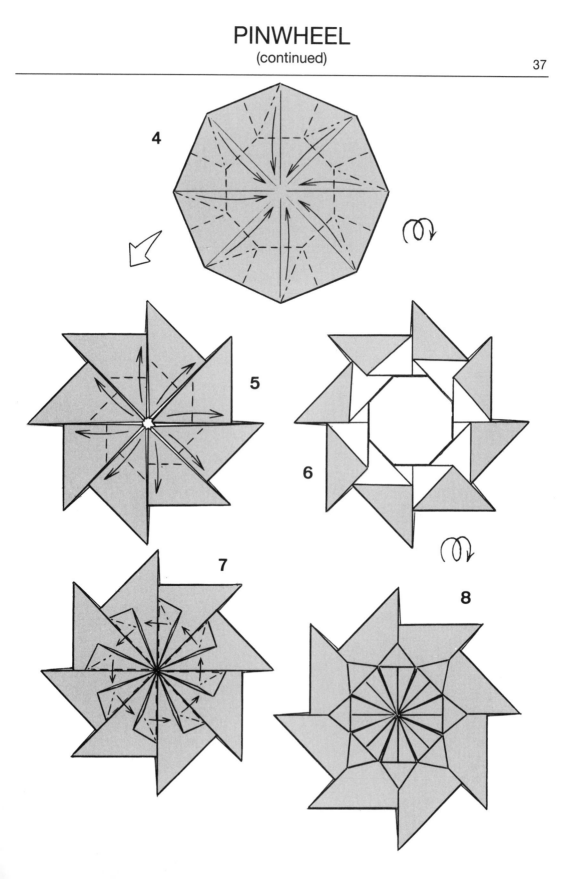

CHECKED BOX 5
by Francisco J. Caboblanco

✳ ✳

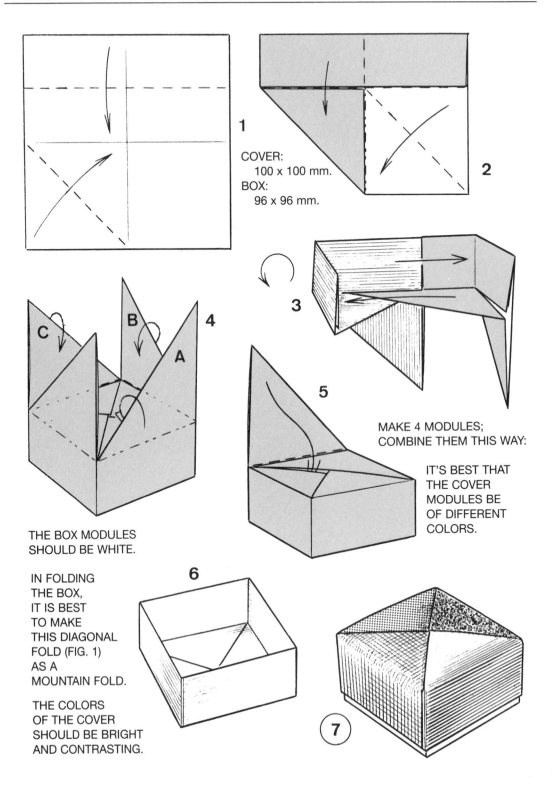

1

COVER:
    100 x 100 mm.
BOX:
    96 x 96 mm.

2

3

4

C   B
    A

5

MAKE 4 MODULES;
COMBINE THEM THIS WAY:

IT'S BEST THAT
THE COVER
MODULES BE
OF DIFFERENT
COLORS.

THE BOX MODULES
SHOULD BE WHITE.

IN FOLDING
THE BOX,
IT IS BEST
TO MAKE
THIS DIAGONAL
FOLD (FIG. 1)
AS A
MOUNTAIN FOLD.

THE COLORS
OF THE COVER
SHOULD BE BRIGHT
AND CONTRASTING.

6

7

TRIANGULAR BOX WITH COVER
by Francisco J. Caboblanco

✳ ✳

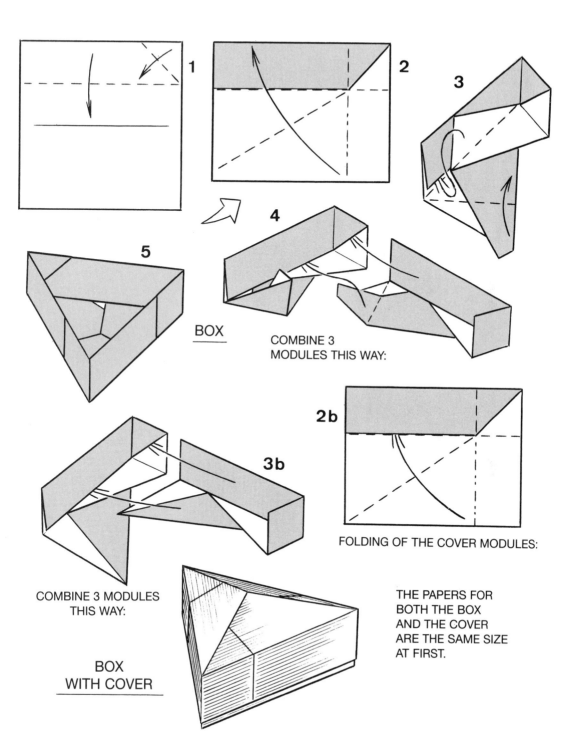

BOX

COMBINE 3
MODULES THIS WAY:

FOLDING OF THE COVER MODULES:

COMBINE 3 MODULES
THIS WAY:

BOX
WITH COVER

THE PAPERS FOR
BOTH THE BOX
AND THE COVER
ARE THE SAME SIZE
AT FIRST.

CHECKED BOX 6
by Francisco J. Caboblanco

* *

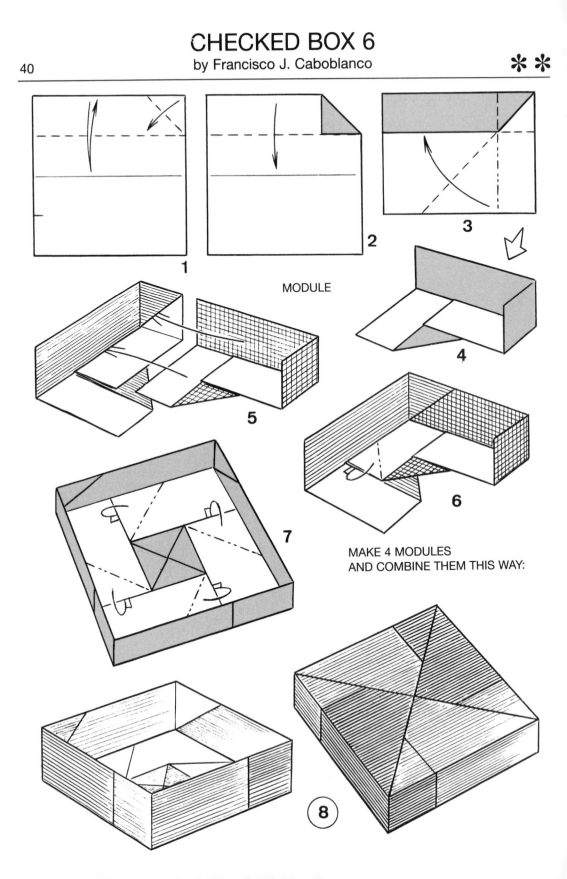

MODULE

MAKE 4 MODULES
AND COMBINE THEM THIS WAY:

BOX-TABLE
by José Krooshoop

✳ ✳ ✳

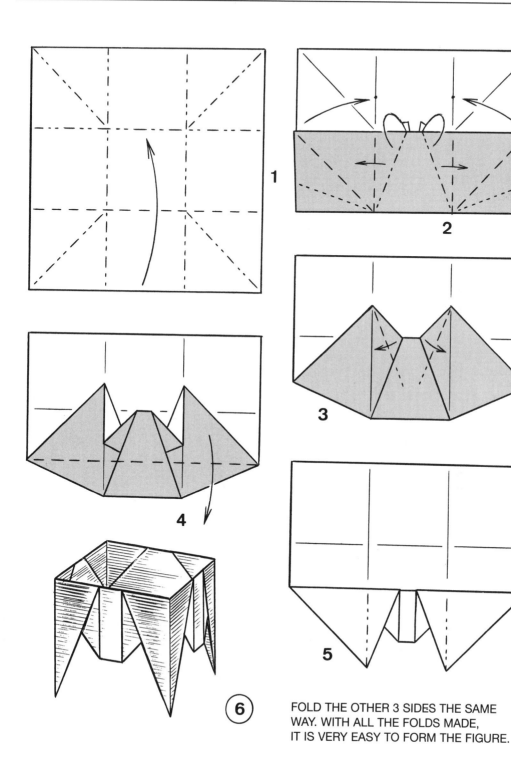

6 FOLD THE OTHER 3 SIDES THE SAME
WAY. WITH ALL THE FOLDS MADE,
IT IS VERY EASY TO FORM THE FIGURE.

TALL BOX WITH COVER
by Francisco J. Caboblanco

✳ ✳ ✳

THE COVER

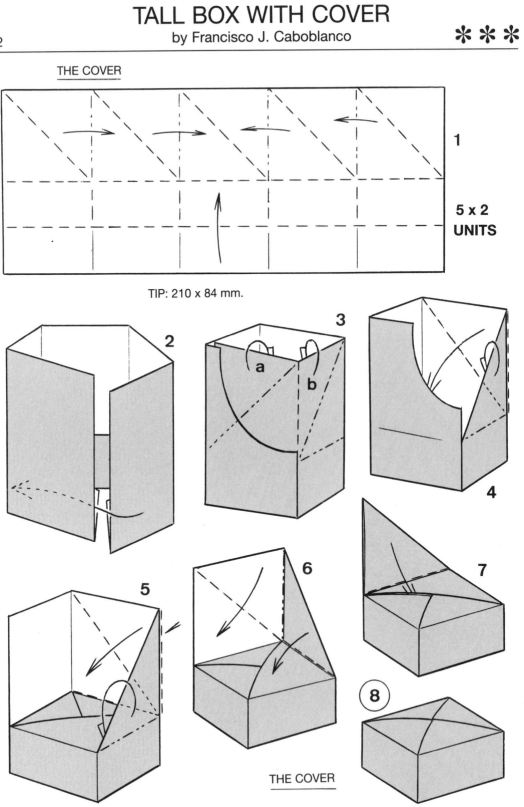

1

5 x 2 UNITS

TIP: 210 x 84 mm.

THE COVER

THE BOX

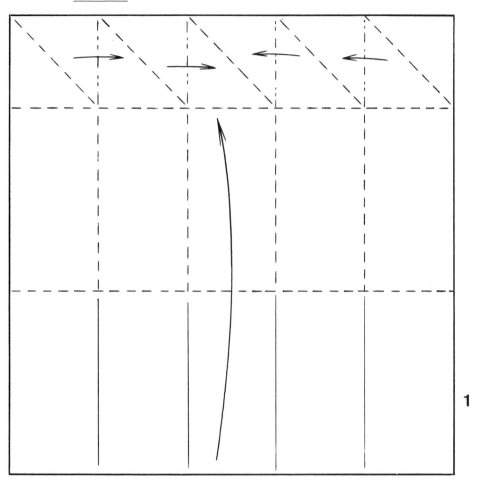

1

TIP: 200 x 200 mm.

THE METHOD OF FOLDING
IS LIKE THAT FOR THE
COVER SHOWN ON THE
PAGE OPPOSITE.

THE COVER,
THE BOX,
AND THE COVERED BOX

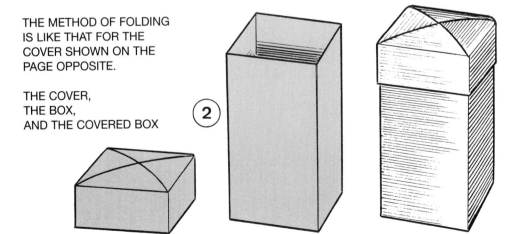

②

BASKET
by Vicente Palacios

✳✳

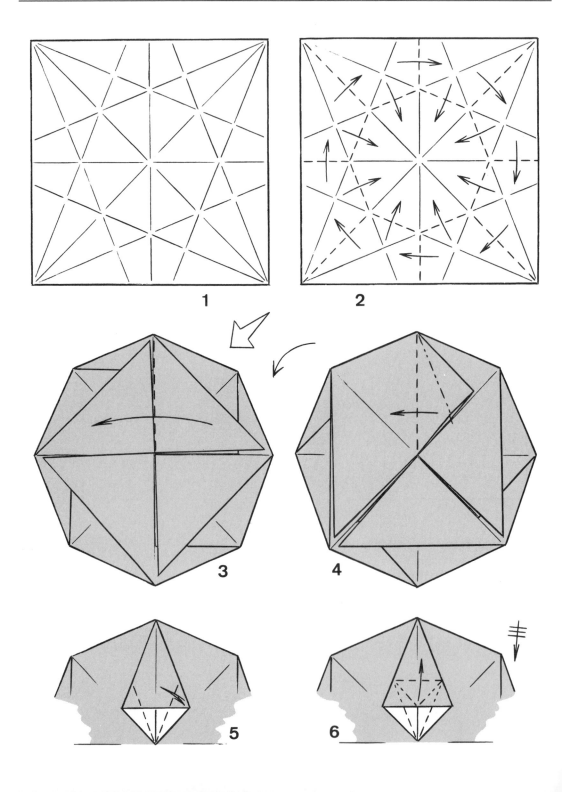

1

2

3

4

5

6

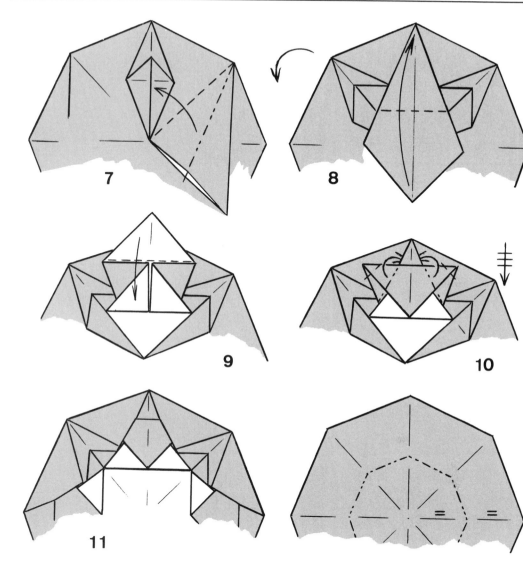

7

8

9

10

11

12

13

ROTATED BOX 1
by Miguel Ángel Palacios

✳ ✳ ✳

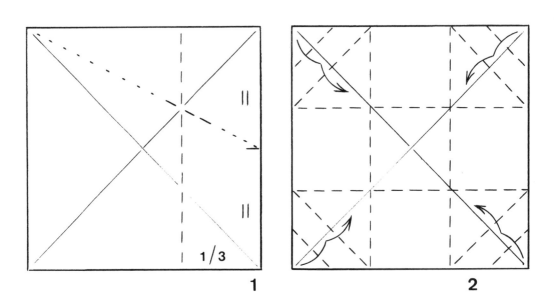

1

2

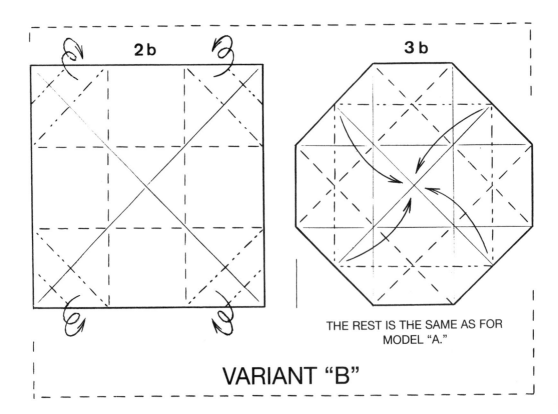

2 b

3 b

THE REST IS THE SAME AS FOR MODEL "A."

VARIANT "B"

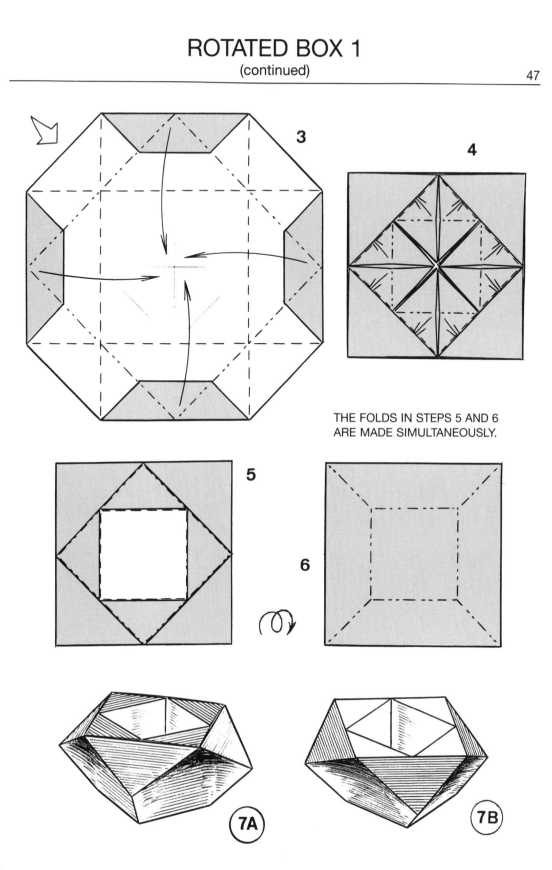

3

4

THE FOLDS IN STEPS 5 AND 6
ARE MADE SIMULTANEOUSLY.

5

6

7A

7B

FIVE-POINTED STAR
by Francisco J. Caboblanco

✳ ✳ ✳

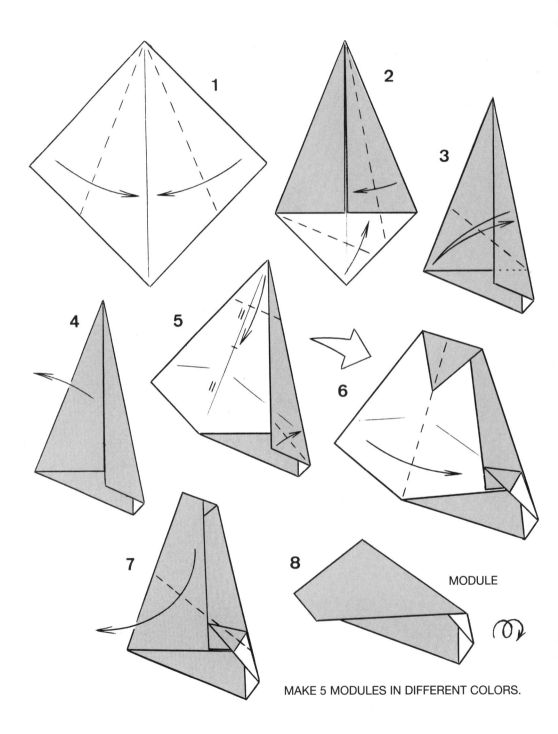

MODULE

MAKE 5 MODULES IN DIFFERENT COLORS.

FIVE-POINTED STAR
(continued)

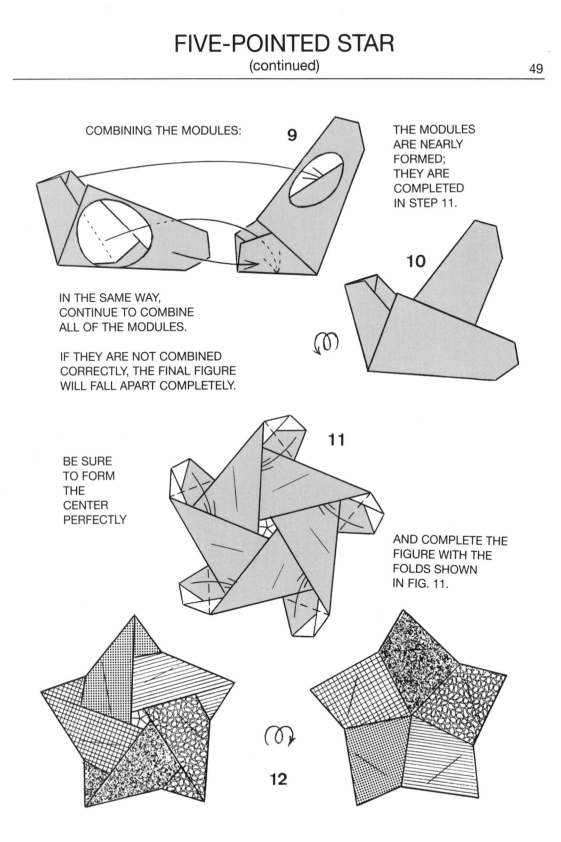

COMBINING THE MODULES:

9

THE MODULES
ARE NEARLY
FORMED;
THEY ARE
COMPLETED
IN STEP 11.

IN THE SAME WAY,
CONTINUE TO COMBINE
ALL OF THE MODULES.

IF THEY ARE NOT COMBINED
CORRECTLY, THE FINAL FIGURE
WILL FALL APART COMPLETELY.

10

BE SURE
TO FORM
THE
CENTER
PERFECTLY

11

AND COMPLETE THE
FIGURE WITH THE
FOLDS SHOWN
IN FIG. 11.

12

EIGHT-POINTED STAR 2
by Francisco J. Caboblanco

✳ ✳ ✳

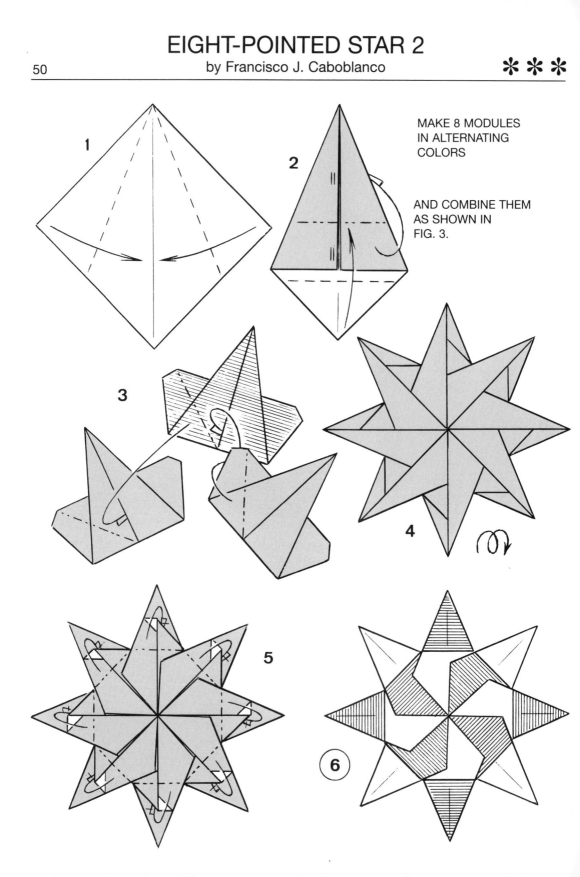

MAKE 8 MODULES
IN ALTERNATING
COLORS

AND COMBINE THEM
AS SHOWN IN
FIG. 3.

STAR WITH WINGS
by Francisco J. Caboblanco

✳ ✳ ✳

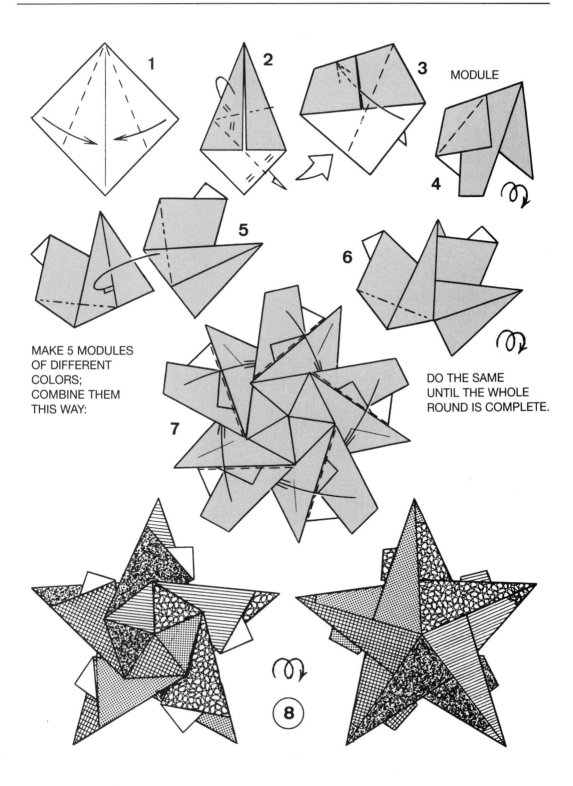

MAKE 5 MODULES
OF DIFFERENT
COLORS;
COMBINE THEM
THIS WAY:

DO THE SAME
UNTIL THE WHOLE
ROUND IS COMPLETE.

MODULE

ROTOR
by Francisco J. Caboblanco

✳ ✳ ✳

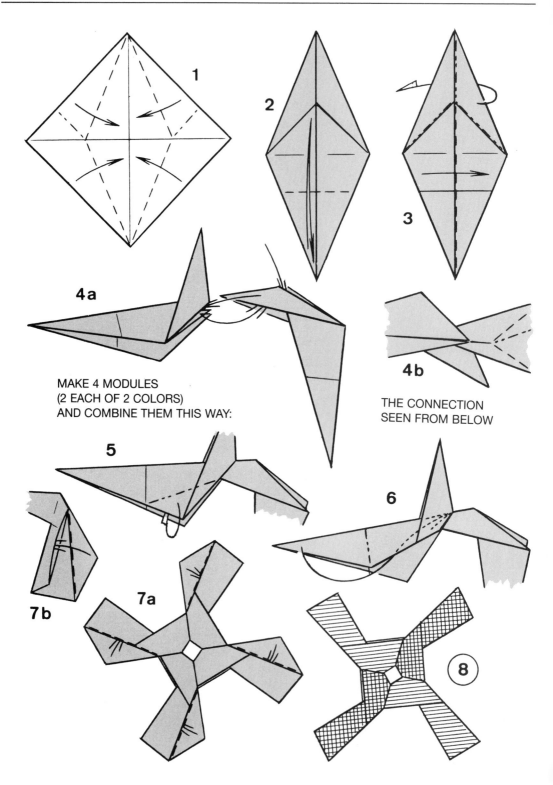

1

2

3

4a

MAKE 4 MODULES
(2 EACH OF 2 COLORS)
AND COMBINE THEM THIS WAY:

4b

THE CONNECTION
SEEN FROM BELOW

5

6

7b

7a

8

MODULAR WHEEL
by Francisco J. Caboblanco

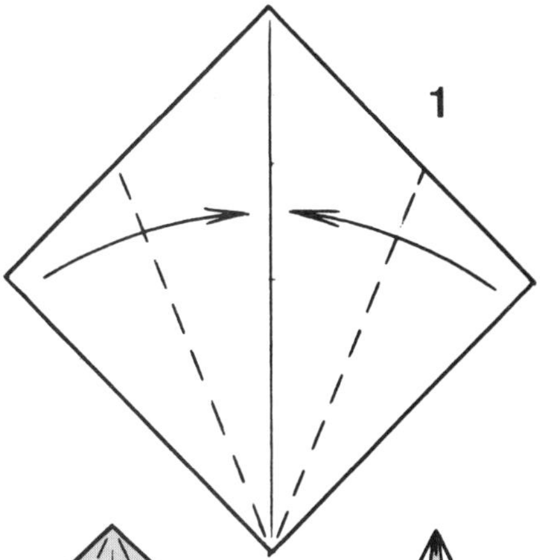

* * *

1

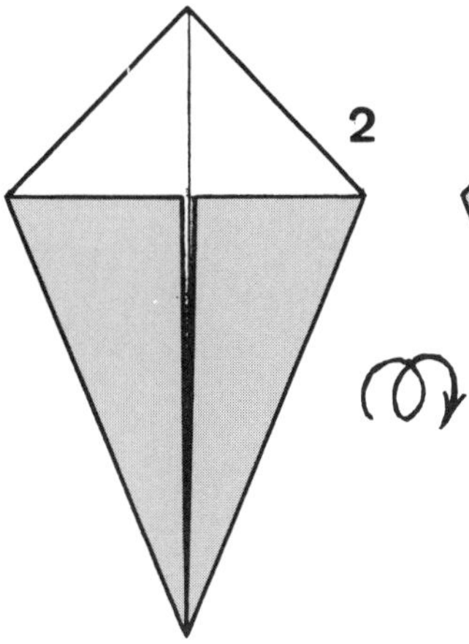

2

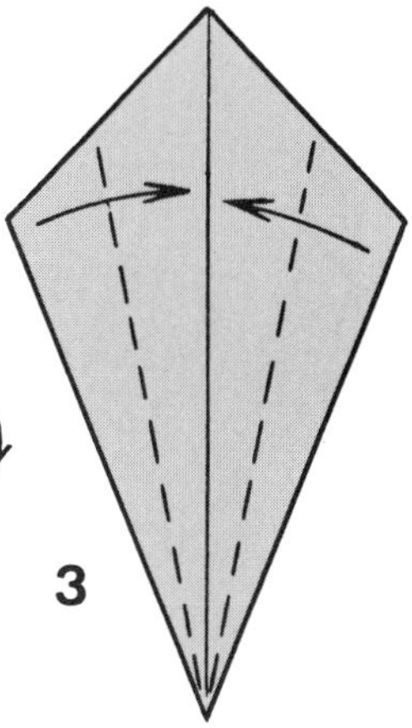

3

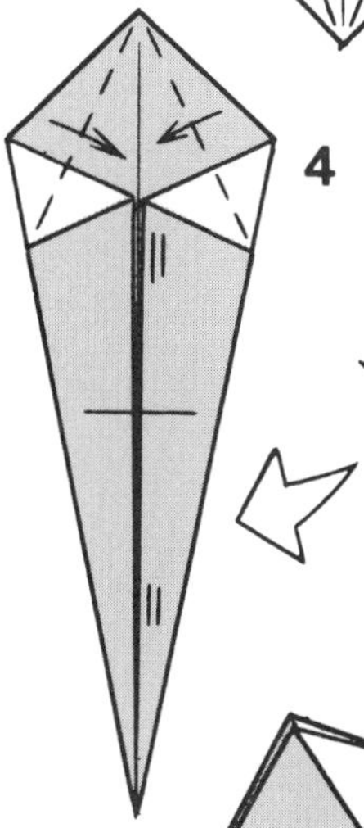

4

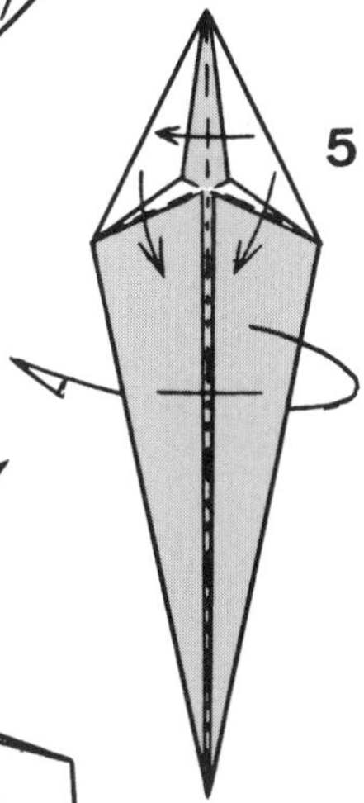

5

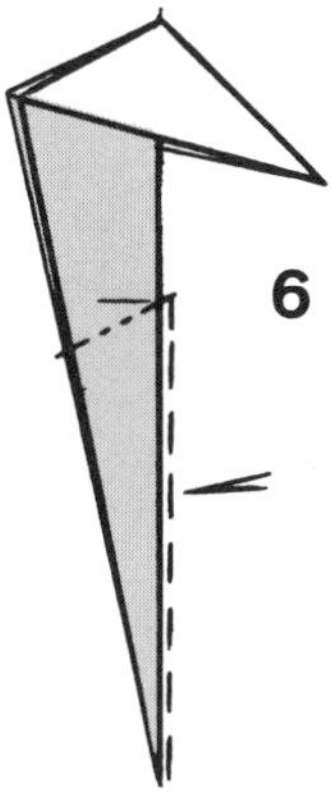

6

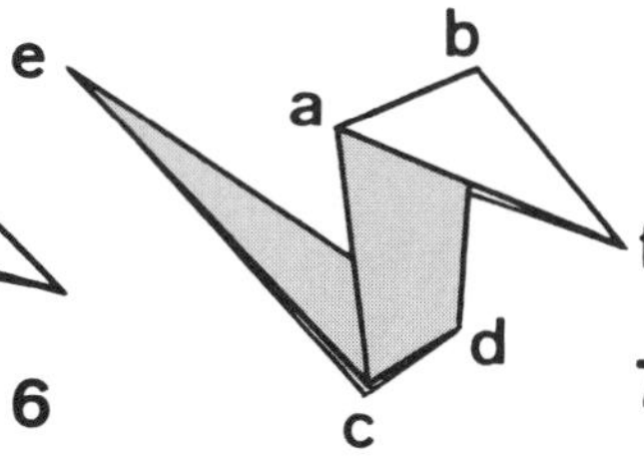

e

a

b

f

d

c

7

MODULE

Note that **ab**
is parallel to **cd**

and that **bf**
is parallel to **ec**.

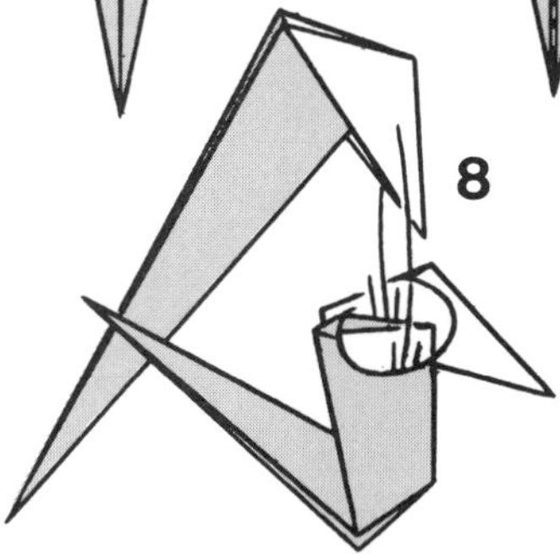

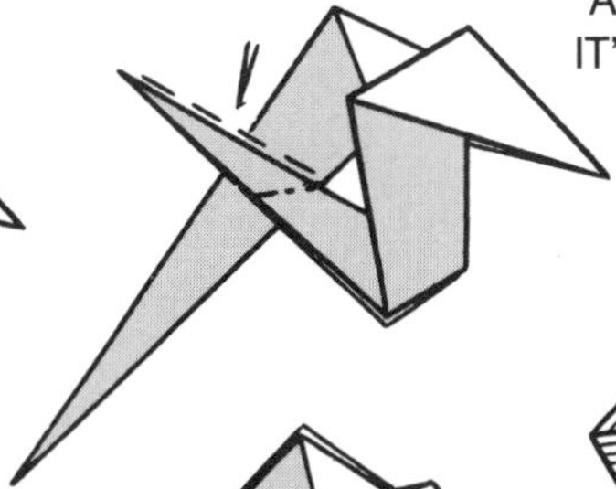

COMBINE THE 8 MODULES,
AS IN FIG. 11, ALL AROUND.
IT'S BEST TO USE TWEEZERS
TO FINISH.

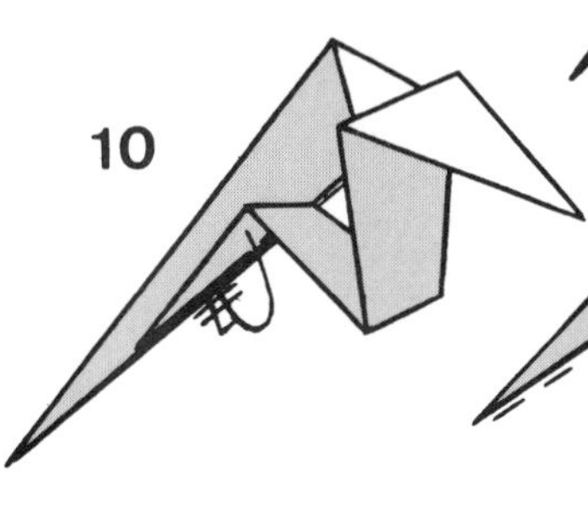

8

9

10

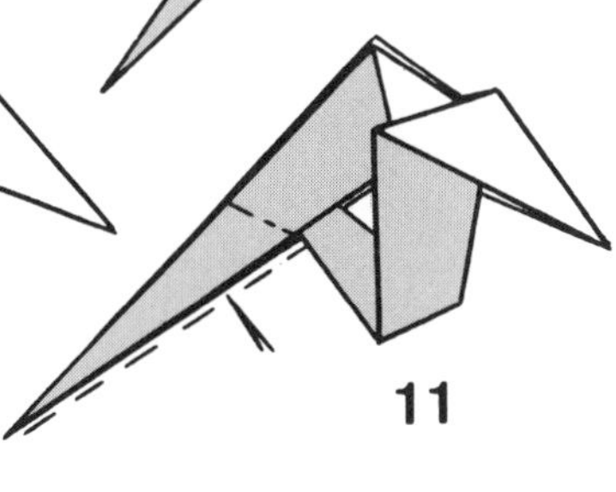

11

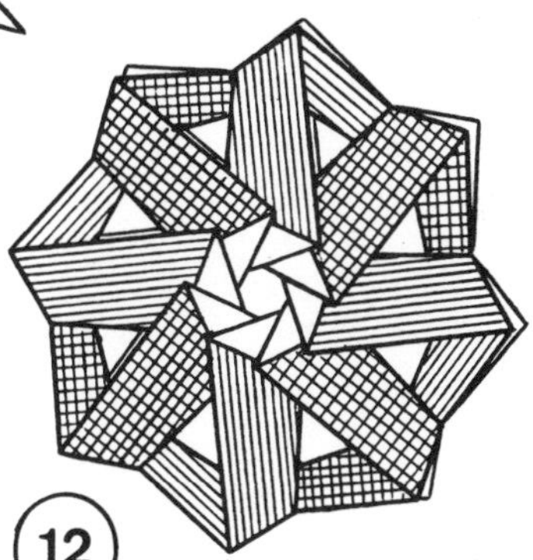

12

EASTER DISH
by José Krooshoop

✳ ✳ ✳

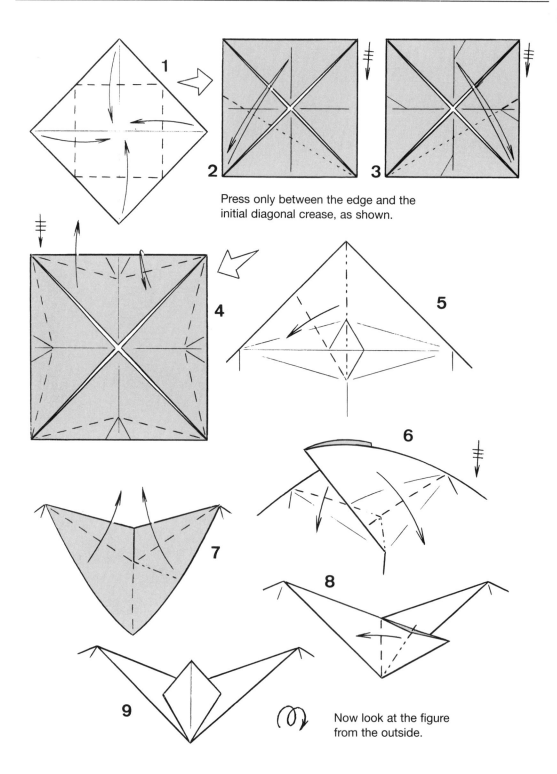

Press only between the edge and the initial diagonal crease, as shown.

Now look at the figure from the outside.

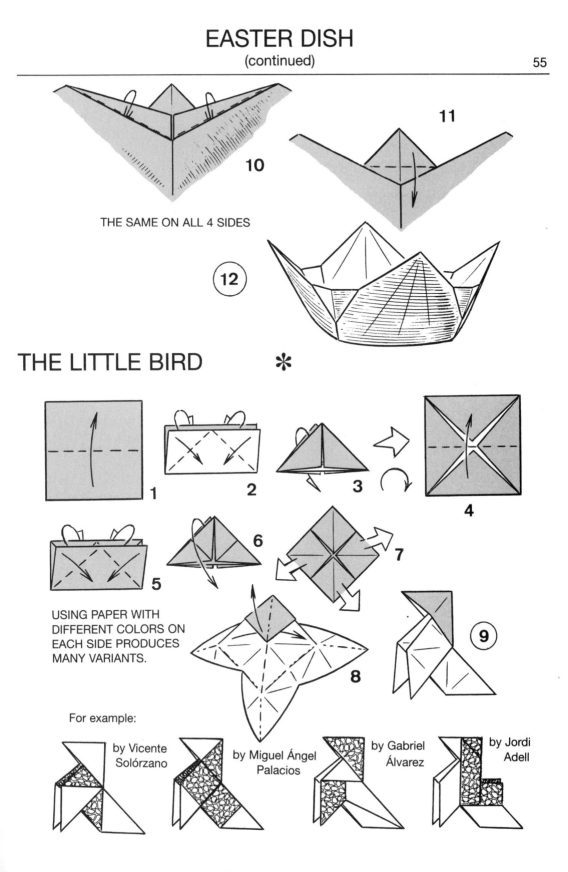

10

THE SAME ON ALL 4 SIDES

11

12

THE LITTLE BIRD ✱

1

2

3

4

5

6

7

8

9

USING PAPER WITH
DIFFERENT COLORS ON
EACH SIDE PRODUCES
MANY VARIANTS.

For example:

by Vicente
Solórzano

by Miguel Ángel
Palacios

by Gabriel
Álvarez

by Jordi
Adell

DISPLAY CASE
by Francisco J. Caboblanco

✳ ✳ ✳

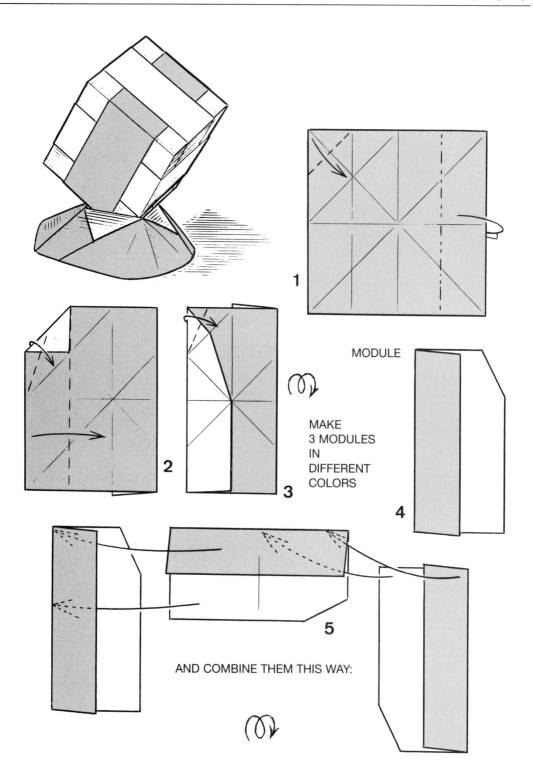

1

2

3

MAKE
3 MODULES
IN
DIFFERENT
COLORS

MODULE

4

5

AND COMBINE THEM THIS WAY:

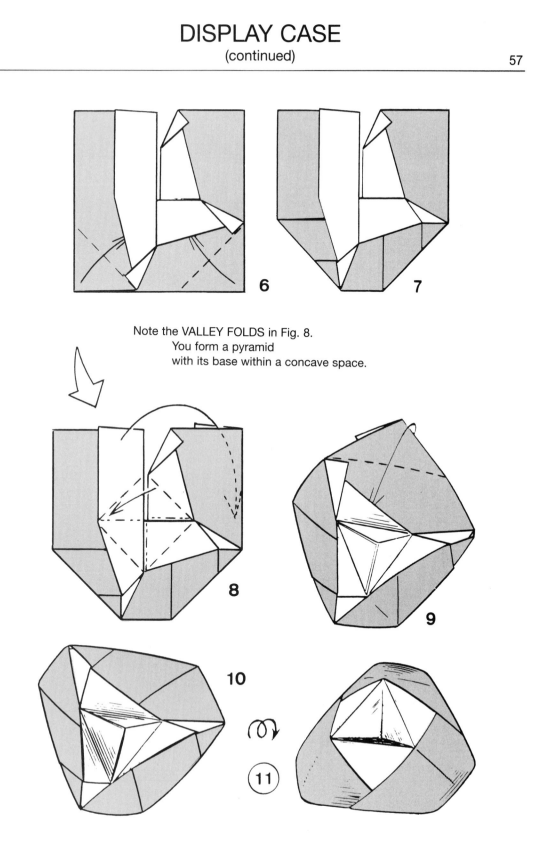

6

7

Note the VALLEY FOLDS in Fig. 8.
You form a pyramid
with its base within a concave space.

8

9

10

11

EIGHT-SIDED BOX

Variant of a Famous Vase
(discovered in Hong Kong)

✳ ✳ ✳

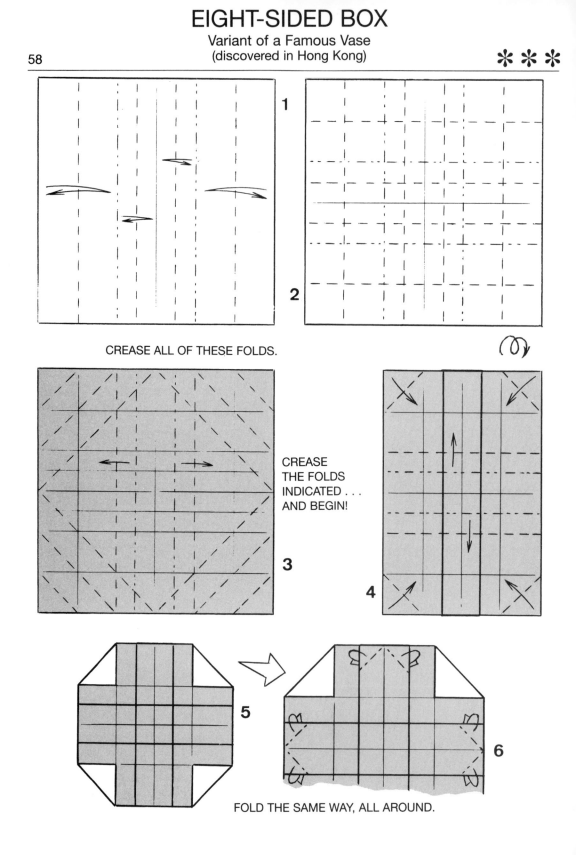

CREASE ALL OF THESE FOLDS.

CREASE
THE FOLDS
INDICATED . . .
AND BEGIN!

FOLD THE SAME WAY, ALL AROUND.

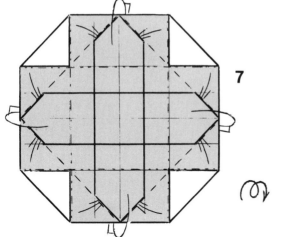

7

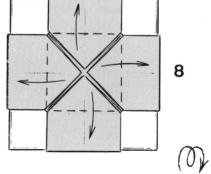

8

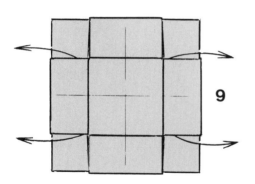

9

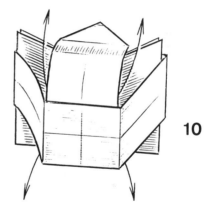

10

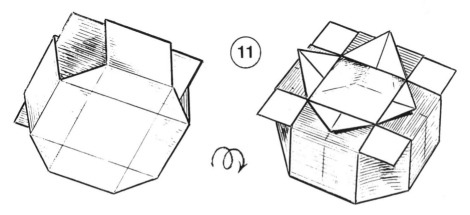

11

✳ ✳

THE COVER

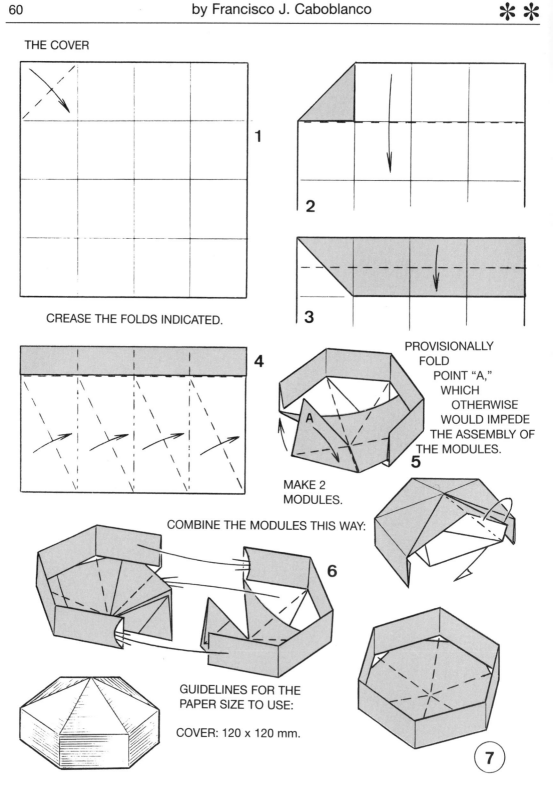

1

2

3

CREASE THE FOLDS INDICATED.

4

PROVISIONALLY
FOLD
POINT "A,"
WHICH
OTHERWISE
WOULD IMPEDE
THE ASSEMBLY OF
THE MODULES.

5

MAKE 2
MODULES.

COMBINE THE MODULES THIS WAY:

6

GUIDELINES FOR THE
PAPER SIZE TO USE:

COVER: 120 x 120 mm.

7

THE BOX

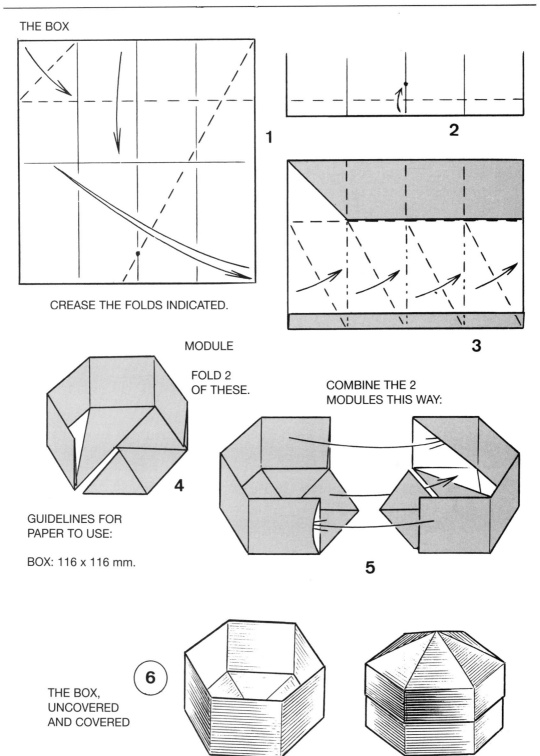

CREASE THE FOLDS INDICATED.

1

2

3

MODULE

FOLD 2
OF THESE.

4

COMBINE THE 2
MODULES THIS WAY:

5

GUIDELINES FOR
PAPER TO USE:

BOX: 116 x 116 mm.

6

THE BOX,
UNCOVERED
AND COVERED

TEN-SIDED BOX
by Francisco J. Caboblanco

✳ ✳ ✳

TWO PAPERS:

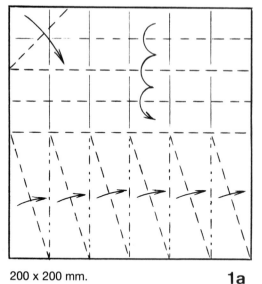

200 x 200 mm.

1a

TWO PAPERS:

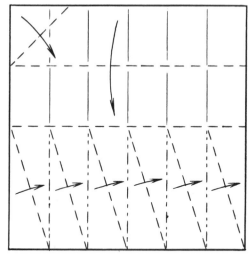

195 x 195 mm.

1b

FOLLOWING THE PROCEDURES FOR
THE PRECEDING LITTLE BOX,
AND USING THE FOLDS INDICATED,
MAKE THE COVER WITH 2 MODULES,
AND THE BOX ITSELF WITH THE OTHER 2.

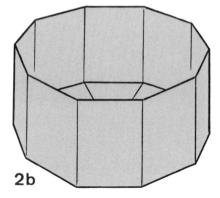

2b

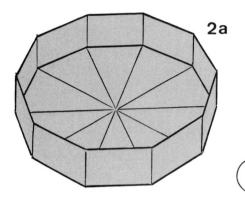

2a

COMBINING THE 2 MODULES, FOR THE
COVER AS WELL AS FOR THE BOX, IS
MUCH EASIER IF YOU BEGIN BY JOINING
EACH PAIR OF MODULES, ON THE OTHER SIDE
OF THE FIGURE.

3

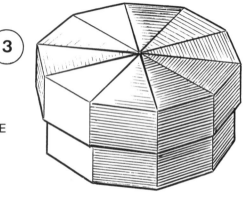

WHISTLE THAT WHISTLES
by Ángel Écija

**

DRAW THE LINES IN FIG. 1 IN PENCIL ON THE CARDBOARD
BEFORE BEGINNING TO FOLD.

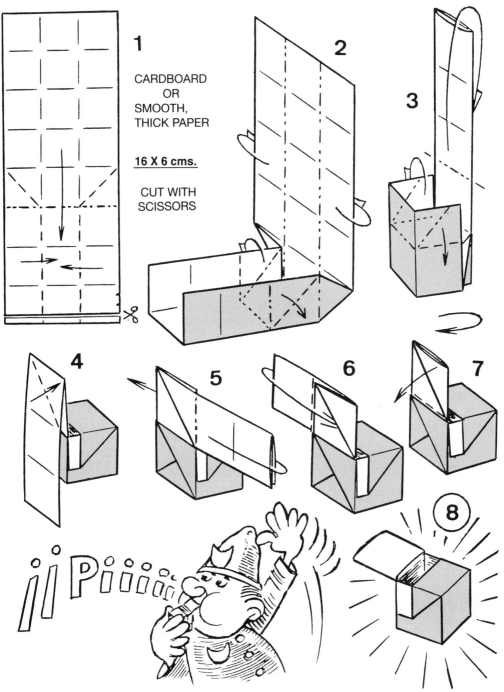

1

CARDBOARD
OR
SMOOTH,
THICK PAPER

16 X 6 cms.

CUT WITH
SCISSORS

2

3

4

5

6

7

8

¡¡Piiiiiii...!!

CINDERELLA'S SHOE
by Yoshihide Momotani

✳ ✳ ✳ ✳

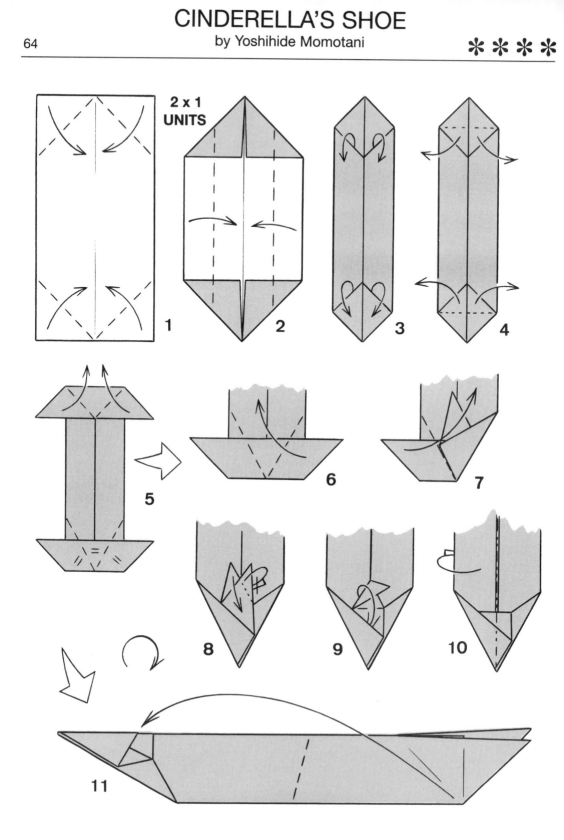

2 x 1 UNITS

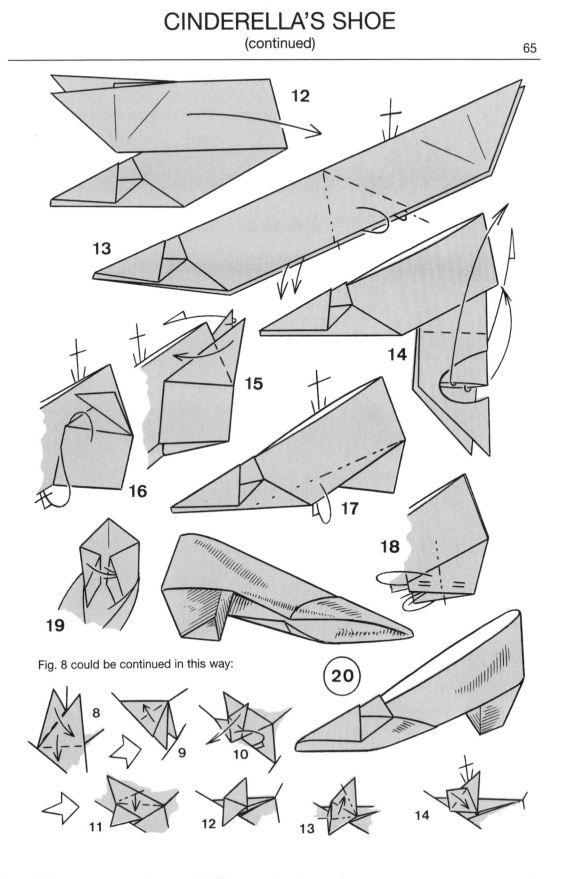

Fig. 8 could be continued in this way:

GYROSCOPE 1
by Francisco J. Caboblanco

✳✳✳✳

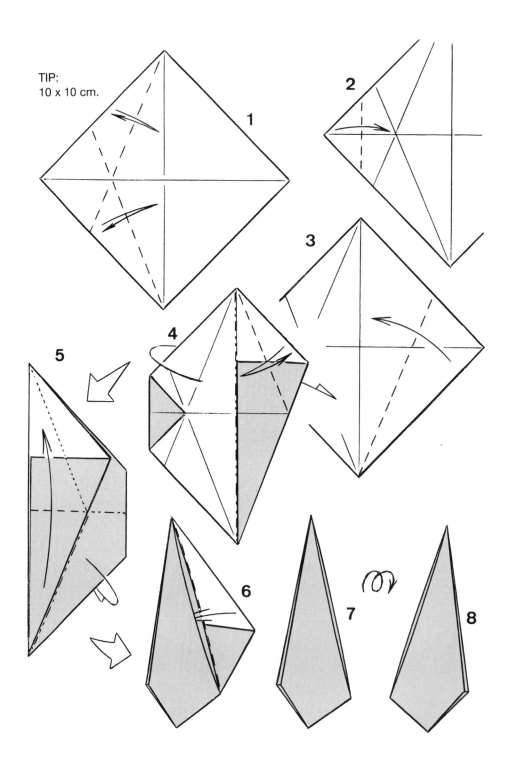

TIP:
10 x 10 cm.

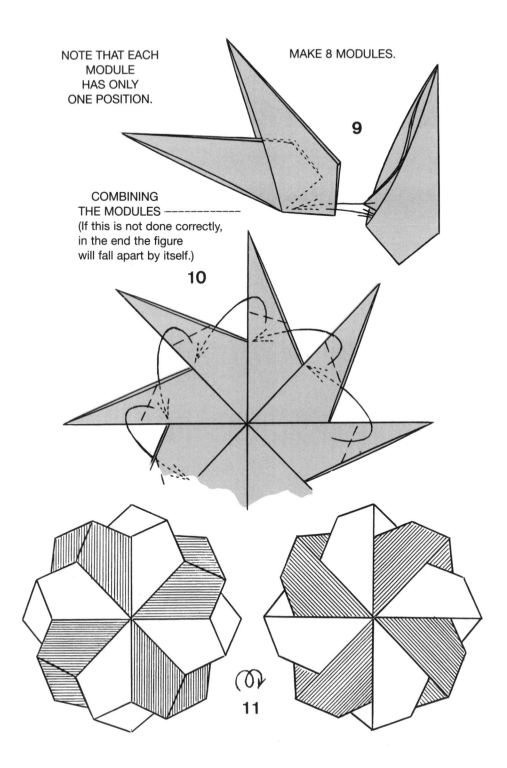

NOTE THAT EACH
MODULE
HAS ONLY
ONE POSITION.

MAKE 8 MODULES.

9

COMBINING
THE MODULES ———————
(If this is not done correctly,
in the end the figure
will fall apart by itself.)

10

11

GYROSCOPE 2
by Francisco J. Caboblanco

✳ ✳ ✳ ✳

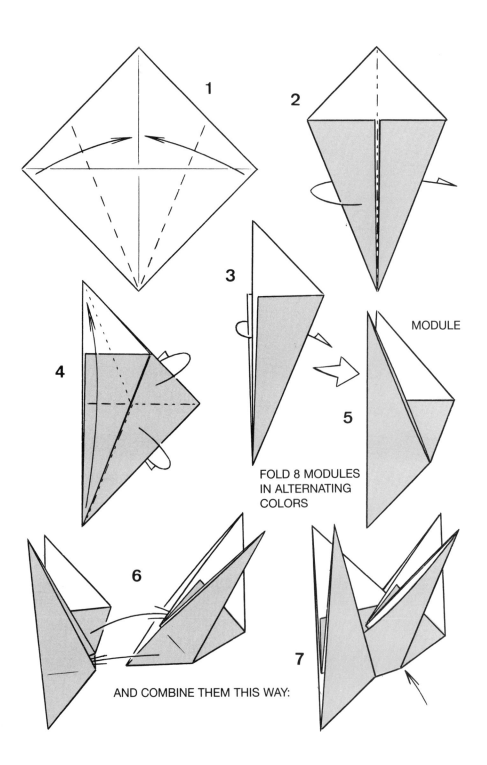

MODULE

FOLD 8 MODULES
IN ALTERNATING
COLORS

AND COMBINE THEM THIS WAY:

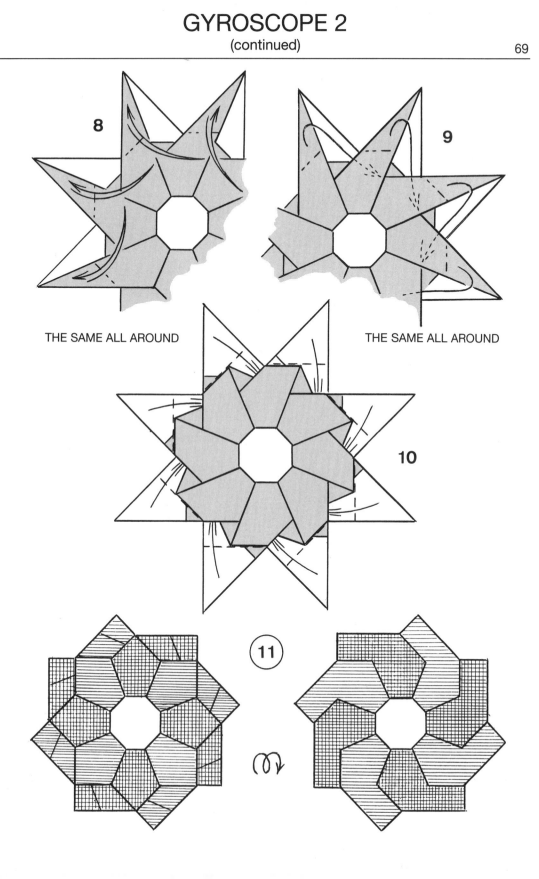

8

9

THE SAME ALL AROUND

THE SAME ALL AROUND

10

11

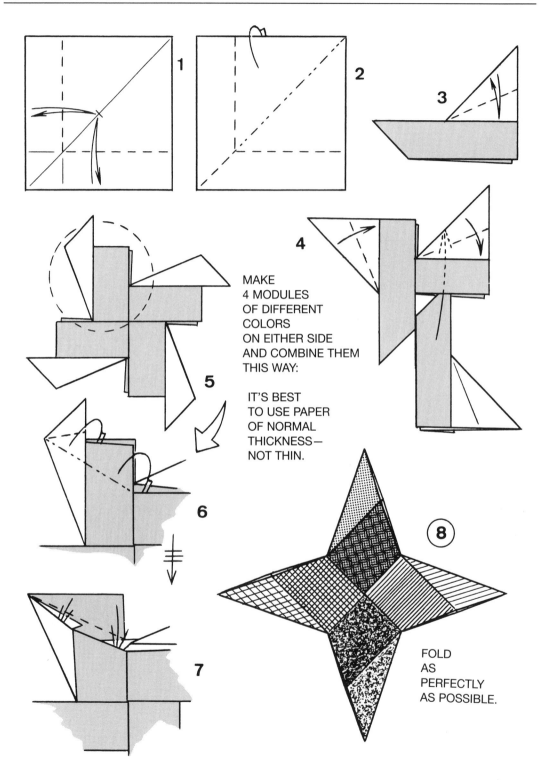

MAKE
4 MODULES
OF DIFFERENT
COLORS
ON EITHER SIDE
AND COMBINE THEM
THIS WAY:

IT'S BEST
TO USE PAPER
OF NORMAL
THICKNESS—
NOT THIN.

FOLD
AS
PERFECTLY
AS POSSIBLE.

ROTATED BOX 2 AND THREE VARIANTS

✽ ✽ ✽ ✽ by Miguel Ángel Palacios

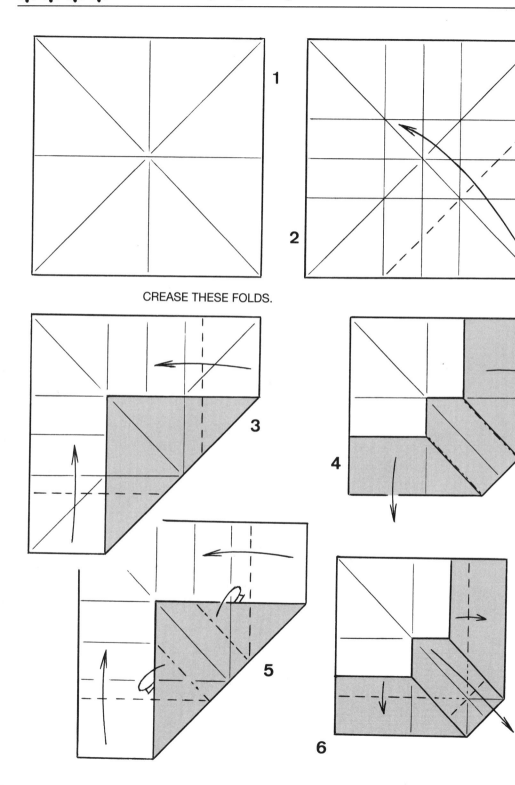

CREASE THESE FOLDS.

UNFOLD EVERYTHING. REPEAT THE FOLDS
SUCCESSIVELY AT EACH OF THE 4 CORNERS.
ONCE THE FOLDS ARE CREASED,
FOLD THE 4 CORNERS
AT THE
SAME TIME.

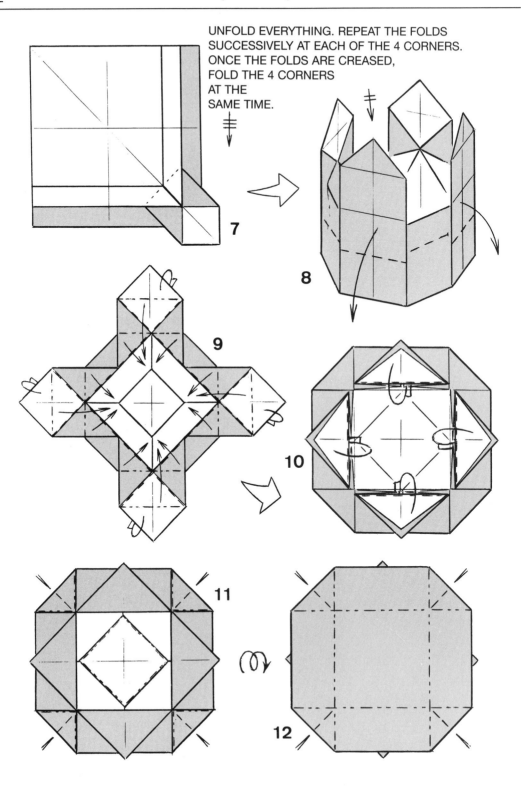

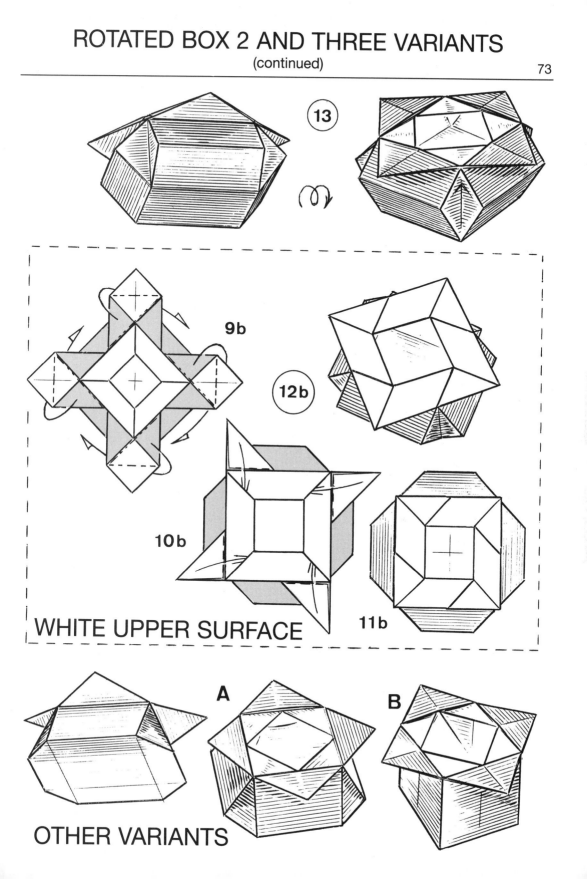

13

9b

12b

10b

11b

WHITE UPPER SURFACE

A

B

OTHER VARIANTS

DOUBLE MEASURE
by Francisco J. Caboblanco

✻ ✻ ✻ ✻

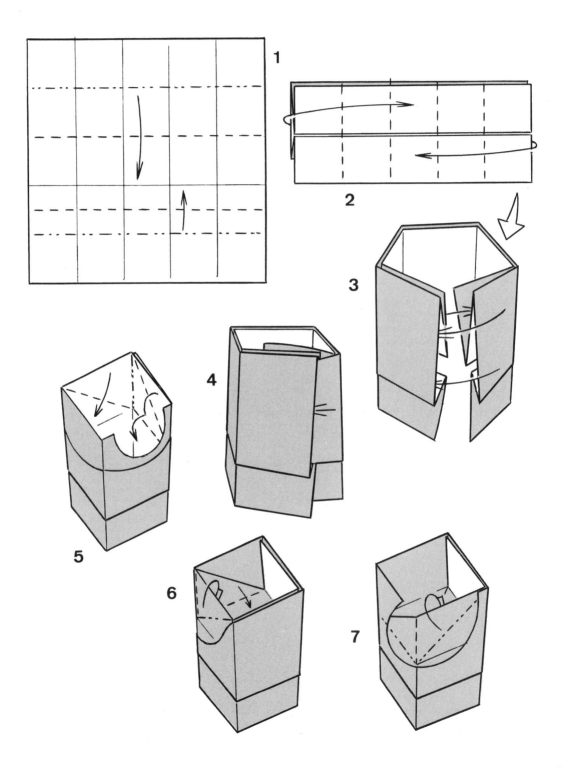

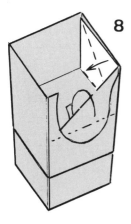

8

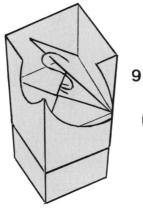

9

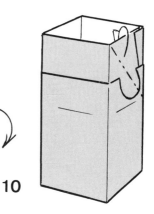

10

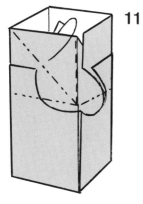

11

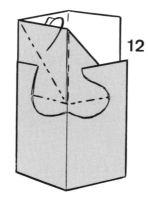

12

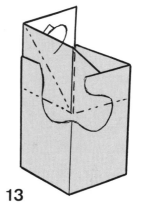

13

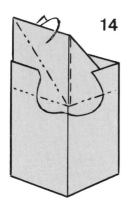

14

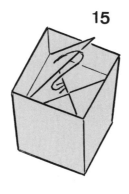

15

16

THREE-DIMENSIONAL STAR
by Francisco J. Caboblanco

✳ ✳ ✳ ✳

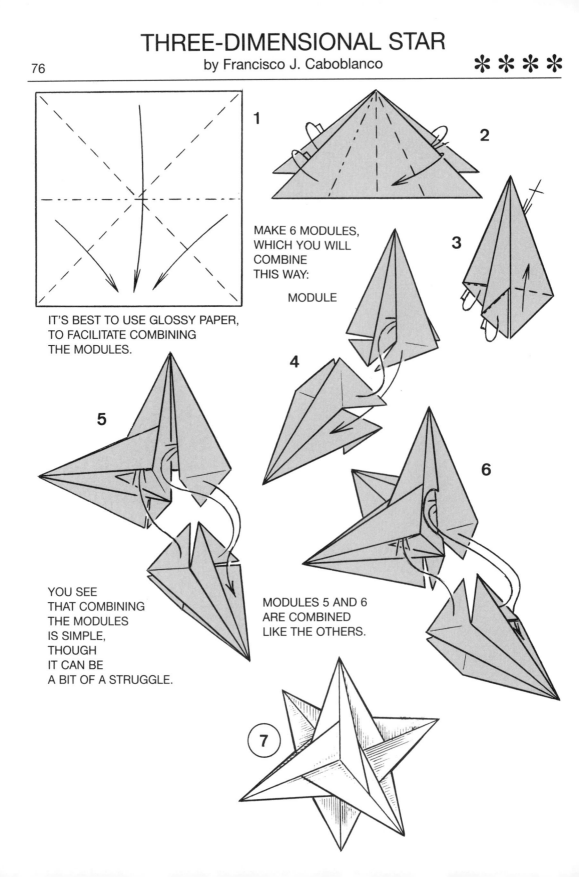

IT'S BEST TO USE GLOSSY PAPER,
TO FACILITATE COMBINING
THE MODULES.

MAKE 6 MODULES,
WHICH YOU WILL
COMBINE
THIS WAY:

MODULE

YOU SEE
THAT COMBINING
THE MODULES
IS SIMPLE,
THOUGH
IT CAN BE
A BIT OF A STRUGGLE.

MODULES 5 AND 6
ARE COMBINED
LIKE THE OTHERS.

✳ ✳ ✳ ✳

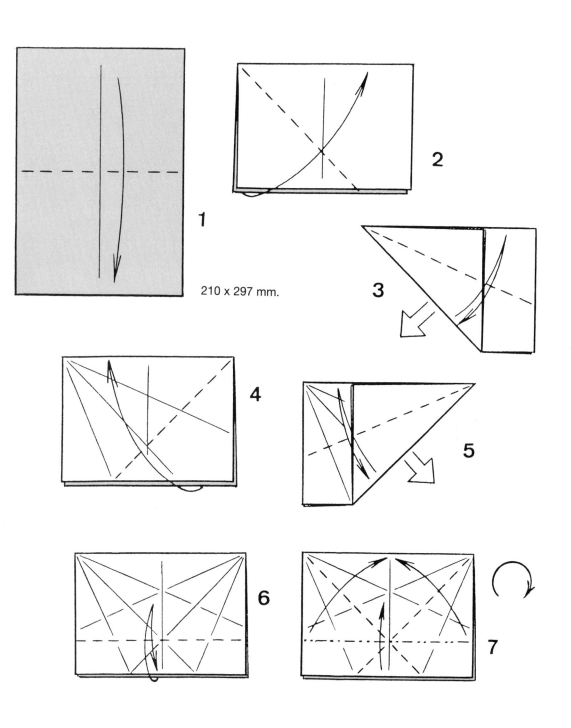

210 x 297 mm.

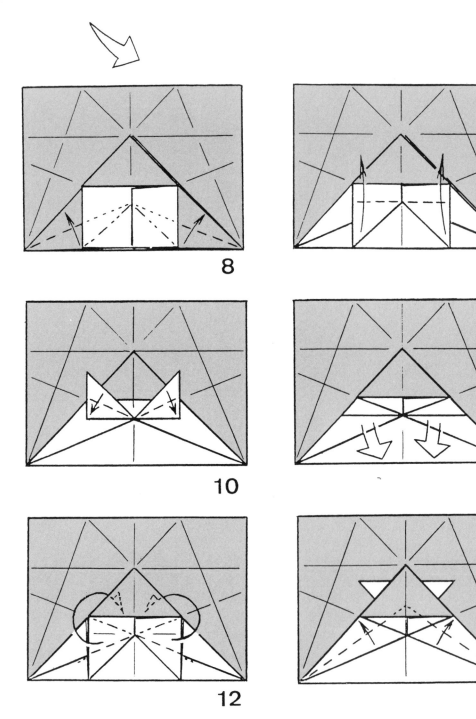

8

9

10

11

12

13

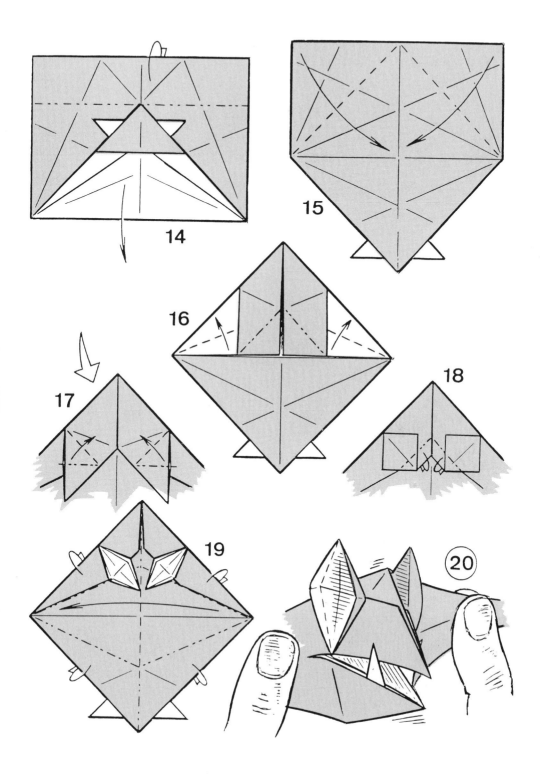

FLOWERPOT
by Ángel Écija

✳ ✳ ✳ ✳

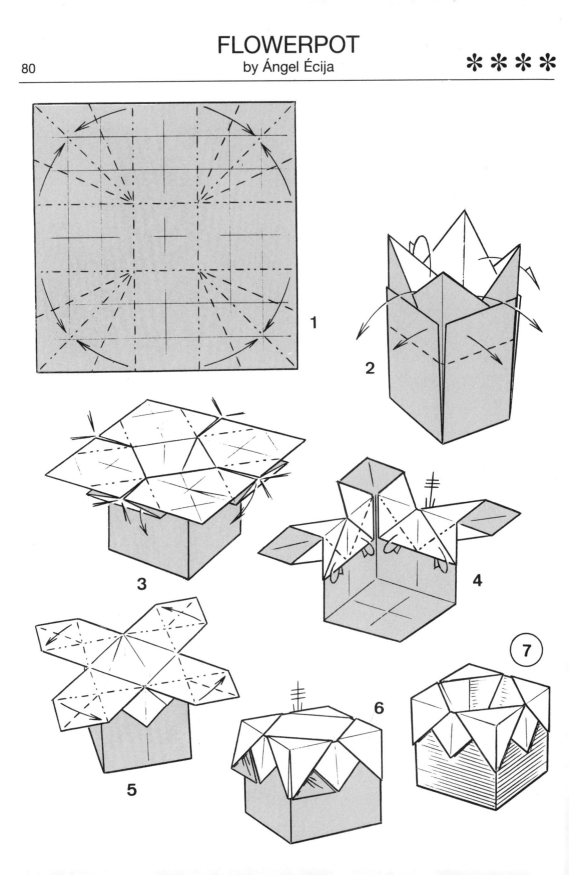